T0148643

MY LIFE:
A BEGINNING THAT LED TO THE REALIZATION OF GOD'S LOVE

An Autobiography of Bishop
Dr. Carolyn D. Arnett

CAROLYN ARNETT

Print information available on the last page.

ISBN: 978-1-4907-4692-0 (sc)
ISBN: 978-1-4907-4691-3 (e)

Library of Congress Control Number: 2014916648

Trafford rev. 06/30/2015

 www.trafford.com

North America & international
toll-free: 1 888 232 4444 (USA & Canada)
fax: 812 355 4082

Contents

DEDICATION

This book is dedicated to the memory of my grandmother who loved me in spite of my looks. To my grand-baby Jacob who show me how to live and die. To my dearly beloved sweet mother who raised, inspired and encouraged me to never give up and to always strive to do the very best that I could. To my younger of my older brothers who has recently died. May they all rest in God's Peace. And to my loving and devoted husband and children and grandchildren who all in some way encouraged me to finish the book!!

FOREWORD

I never intended for this to be a chapter book. I wanted it to be one long story as the pages reveal steps that my life took as my story unfolds, one of reflections and thought patterns. It is my hope that you look at the outline as an aid to what I am trying to convey rather than a chapter by chapter process.

The Book is based on the Mercies of God found in these scriptures: Psalm 145:8,9 out of which I am inspired to write this book from the depths of my heart for the love of God's people and the love that God. (The Father, The Son and The Holy Spirit) has shown and instilled in me through their great mercies bestowed upon me while on this journey.

My prayer is that this book will enlighten you and encourage you to fall in love with God more than ever before by seeing and reading my life experiences that your faith will increase and help you to appreciate salvation, make God more real to your struggle in life and assure you that God can change and use you, an ordinary person in an extraordinary way.

I want to express in this book the Mercies, God has allowed me to partake and enjoy over the years I have been on this planet earth. God's mercies have always been with me even when I was unaware and without understanding that there were mercies. I cannot imagine my life without God at this point. Scriptures tells us that God's mercies are a fresh and a new each day. Lamentations 3:22-23 And "His mercy is everlasting", Psalm 100:5, "His mercy endureth for ever". Psalm 136. God's word lets us know we don't have to stumble and fall while on this life journey but if we do/when we do God's mercy is ever presence to help us back on our feet. For God is our present help in time of need(Psalm 46:1. As I am writing this book God the Holy Spirit instructs me do do all in love. So what may be said or expressed in this book is not out of hatred or vindictiveness or revenge or any other adjective that might be thought of. I am prayerful and cautious of the writings of this book, while trying to be true to myself.

This book is not one of those tell all books, just because I can, because some of the things I have written breaks my heart and causes me to shudder even now and maybe even run and hide in a closet to think I have done these things or brought regret to my God. But God has forgiven me and reached out to me with His faithfulness showing me love and kindness.

I must say what appeared to be a normal run of the mill family, was truly a dysfunctional family now that I have had time to reflect. My childhood happy home was not so happy or good times were not so good. This is an attempt to show how God can work even in a dysfunctional family I feel we as children made a contribution to society and did our far share to hold things in perspective as best we knew how. This encounter of the past times, struggles and hardships I encountered alone the way; some that was evoked and others I brought on myself by my ignorance. I am not proud of all the things I have done but I am glad to have had the opportunity to experience some good things along the way. I wish somehow I could erase some areas and start over with a clean slate, but how ever I must keep in mind that Through God I have a new life, in a spiritual sense; my slate have been wiped clean, for scriptures states behold you are a new creature in Christ Jesus.

I realize that even though I have been given a fresh start this does not ease the memories nor the consequences of my actions, for God Word is true, we will pay for the deed done in this body and whatsoever seed you have sown you will reap. (Gal.6:7 Ezra 9:13, Romans 8:13 Psalm 28: Job 4:8). Keeping in mind when we turn from our wicked ways: God forgives us and states in the Word "Now therefore there is no condemnation to those who walk upright and love Him" (Roman 8:1).

What makes this book unique is that it's my hope to help someone not to follow down the same pattern of life I've gone. And to share my testimony of the goodness of God as He kept me though all these things: showing how His love never fails no matter what situation we find ourselves in.

God has truly been my very present help in times of need, through sickness and death, pain and misery, hope and fears, disappointments, hurt, divorce, alone but never defeated, Because with God: we are victorious in every area!!! Hallelujah!!!! Like Paul stated knocked down but not forsaken. God has taught me many things. I used my full name Griffin to show an inner healing that had taken place, for a long time it was hard to tell anybody that I was married twice. (I have been married now for 39 years.) God has done so much healing and overhauling in my life, changing my way of thinking and understanding things: I love God so dearly. I want to acknowledge God the Father, God the Son and God the precious Holy Ghost for their ever present help in my life and to be ever mindful that I am an ambassador of Christ and I am truly grateful of what He has done in my life.

I understand now that God has had his hand on my life from the very beginning and called me in my mother's womb. I fully understand that through Jesus coming, death burial and resurrection I have been made an heir to the glorious throne of God. God the Father have adopted me into the kingdom, and God the holy Ghost is leading guiding instructing, directing me along this narrow path of righteousness and we will rejoice together some day with all those who have died in Christ. It is my hope to hear the Master Shepherd and Lord of Lord's and King of King say "Well done good and faithful servant you have been faithful over a few come up to the many. Because God stated to me long years ago:" Be thou faithful until death and I will give you a Crown of Life." Revelation 1:3.

It's my hope that as you read this book you will truly learn how to experience God's love through your everyday life experiences. It's my prayer also that as you read this book you will know God's love and discover how God can be a present help on your life journey. My life is not over yet and I will experience a lot more of God's tender mercies as I travel down this life journey, I Hope you will too!

My Early years

Psalms 119:92

My full name is Carolyn Diane. I was born to my mother and father on August 22nd, 1952 in Memphis Tennessee, in the John Gaston Hospital. I was born 1 month premature weighed 4lbs, but my mom said I was a fighter. I stayed in the hospital for about a month in Hot Springs, until coming home according to my mom weighing only 5 pounds. I was raised in rural Arkansas, outside a small town. I was very small framed, short in height, squint eyes, mousy voice, the homily one of the family. The fifth child of the family for my mom had a still born before me, a boy. I often wonder what he would have been like. And why did he not survive? My mom never had any more children.

My parents names were Mr. Robert Lee and Mrs. Bertha Mae. We were sharecroppers/hired hands. We were a family of six: two older boys and 2 girls. We lived on a farmland owned by a Mr. Frank. His daddy and brother owned land adjacent to his and of course we as children worked and roamed all the land.

My mom a short bright skinned woman stood 4ft 11 inches: she was a very warmhearted person, loving, caring, very hard worker, I remember her carrying me and a bag of cotton on her back up and down the fields. loved everybody people came from miles around to visit us and she welcomed them all. I remember once a family of 5 came to live with us with a small baby, who's mother had died, mom said it was her best friend's baby.

My mother took care of the baby but the baby died too shortly thereafter. I asked my mother why did the baby die:My mother said the baby was lonely for his mother. My dad would bring home strays usually young men all the time. Mom accepted it and made sure there were enough food for all of us to eat. There were one guy named Abraham he stay with us a very long while until finally he moved out to his own place.

This person was like another brother to me, we came to love him as such. I believe I had a crush on him now that I think about it. When hearing of his accident with the tractor where he lost an arm and four fingers from the other hand, burned his face I was so hurt to hear the news. His stay in the hospital was a long one and when he came home to us I was even afraid of him for a while because of what he looked like. My mom was a God fearing woman who took us to church every Sunday. She was also a singer and would be invited to sing on church programs around the community. I went with her almost every time. She established a children's choir at our church where we once attended and we traveled to other churches to sing.

When we became older she would send us on before to attend Sunday school and she would somehow show up later. She taught us to treat everybody the way we wanted to be treated. She worked around the house canning, gardening washing and sterilizing, sewing, and quilting and in the fields chopping, picking cotton, pulling sacks on her back. I would help her as much as I could around the house, for I was too little to be in the fields. My mom could do anything, shot a gun, fish, I believe she could hunt if she had to. The men folk would handle that. The land was good rich soil near the house, where we grew big healthy vegetables. The Family mostly ate from the land and the wild life, when dad would hunt and fish. We truly learned to appreciate the land. My dad and my older brothers were hunters, sometimes they would hunt all night. When they would go hunting we knew we would have something to eat that day and sometimes for days.

My dad was a tall handsome man, a singer and whistler too: he once sung in a quartette, Dad could whistle a tune with exact wording of understanding. He was very stern, a hard working man, drove the farm machinery of all kinds, could hunt, shoot, fish, caught any and everything he went after including women. After his death we discovered that he had 2 extra families.

My dad even though a hard worker, he drank and threw the money away, sometimes to the point of not buying food for us to eat. Sometimes my dad would leave home on Friday evenings and not show up until Monday morning in time for work. Most of the time he showed up he would be drunk, But ready to go to work. I later discovered that he was a functioning alcoholic. He would not beat us only he and mom would argue and they would fight. Once he hit my mom and knocked her off the porch, I believe that changed my feelings toward him, oh I loved him, and I missed him so much when he died, sometimes I still do. I wonder what he would have been like and what would our lives have been like if he had lived. Sometimes I wonder what he would have looked like at an old age. He was killed by one of his lady friends so we were told. Even the police would not help him by calling the ambulance while he laid on the streets dying.

My mom told us stories of how dad would always have them back in the woods far away from everybody and would leave her alone. She said that he had a scream on him that was mighty and boy could run fast! I believe my younger brother and I took after him in that sense. She told us once, he was coming home a very dark night and heard something in the woods and he began to run and hollow then she heard a blimp blimp and he was in the door, she knew he had seem or heard something, she would just laugh after telling the story. She would demonstrate how she imagined him jumping upon the porch.

It appeared that my dad was a loner, depended on no one but himself to provide. I remember him once saying to us we would not borrow, what we did not have we would do without. Now that I thinks about him, I believe that my dad was perhaps a troubled soul, not really having any body to tell his troubles too, except the liquid bottle.

My siblings were all praised: My older brother "Jr." was tall, not so handsome but a true ladies man, a robust kind of guy, a fighter for fun, especially a new boy on the block he would say. The best storyteller in the world, he would tell us stories until we all fell asleep, smart witty, loved to tease, a protector, no one bothered us girls. Remarried for 40 yr.

Once my parents went to town and my older brother started a fire underneath the porch of the house, but by the time it began to burn big my parents came home and my dad put the fire out and gave my brother what I thought was the whipping of his life, we were all scared of getting a whipping that day. My mom told me that she believed that dad was hard on "Jr". because he thought that he wasn't his, while a baby he was high yellow, but changed as he became older. Ooh but if my dad could see him now. I think he looks like him so much.

My second brother, now a preacher: "C boy" was not so tall but handsome, mean spirited seemed to fight us all the time, my older brother would stop him. Sneaky, and stuttered when carrying on a conversation, but never when he preached. He and my older brother seemed to enjoy making us cry, by teasing and doing mischievous things all the time to us and the house. Wife died in December 2012. Now has remarried a sister-in-law of mine. He has died also even before this book could be published.

My sister (whom we all called Booth)she were given that nick-name by our dad; was tall, very pretty, everybody praised her for her looks. She was bright skinned and had dimples, she looked very nice in her clothes, she was very popular with the boys while we was growing up. Even into adulthood, men admired her beauty. My beautiful sister whom now I affectionately call Dee.

And then there were me:My mom would tells us all who we featured and took after and how we got our names. She said I took after my grandmother (my dad's mother) that lived in Florida the dark skinned one. I was short, very thin, had wide shoulders, long arms, bitty eyes, round face, high cheek bones and when I smiled my cheeks would come up to close my eyes to a squint.

I learned to be resourceful from my mom to the best of my ability. I would always find things, dig for things from the ground and old dump piles. I would fish for crayfish (we called them crawdads) and help out around the house, helping my mom can food, gardening and feeding the chickens, pumping water, washing clothes, and other household chores.

Our family was poor but we had some good family times, sitting around a smoke fire, sitting on the porch in the summer and around the potbelly stove in the winter. My mom and dad telling stories, singing old folk songs until time to go to bed. Eating snow cream mother made, when the snow would fall in the winter. We sit around the potbelly stove eating popcorn, my dad was the best popcorn popper in the world.

Growing up in the rural area we had to be resourceful in what we called the country. sometimes the children would pop horse corn ourselves, on the potbelly heater. That's how I burned my leg so badly at age five. Once my older brother's corn popped off the potbelly cast iron heater and he told me to get it. I did but my leg got caught under the heater. I received a third degree burn, which seemed like forever to healed. That event left a huge scar on my leg just above my knee to this today. I got to sleep with mom during my healing because she was afraid my sister would roll over on me an hurt my leg. My sister said I was spoiled.

Sometimes we would put sweet potato in the ask tray of the potbelly heater and let it cook and eat it while it was hot, wow that was good stuff.

We lived in a house up on a hill, this house; people called haunted, after we moved from that house, it mysteriously burned down and no one knew how. We lived in this house when my brother caught the turtle and shove it up to my eye and the turtle bit my eye lid. This was funny to them but I cried, that event left a permanent scar over my eyelid. We were living in this house when my brothers caught a huge logged head snapping turtle. My brother held the attention of that creature until I ran home to get Mr. Grant(ex granddad) a frequent visitor was there. I told him my brother sent me home to get help, so he grab a rifle and he and I ran toward my brothers. Mr. Grant shot the giant turtle and we all were discussing what part that we were going to eat.

Mr. Grant helped us prepare the turtle to eat, I watched him as he cut the body away from the shell and we later used the turtle's shell as a toboggan.

My brothers teased me that the turtle's head was as big as mine, which at that time I did not think it was funny. We also had an event in a boat out on the round pond, the very one our mother told us never to go on to, because there were suppose to be monsters that were big enough to eat you and of course no one will ever find your body. It was also used as a duck hunting place because someone had built a small house in it. But one day my siblings and I decided to go boating in someone's boat on that pond.

We found ourselves in the midst of the pond with our 2 brothers fighting each other, it was a miracle that the boat did not turn over, for Dee and I could not swim. We began to cry, but what saved us that day was when we heard our mother calling for Jr and we heard her voice oh no mom is calling "we got to go", so they stopped fighting and rowed back to the shore as quickly as possible and we ran home of course dad was waiting on us and lined us all up and we got a whipping he just gave me a few licks with his belt because he said if it had not been for them I would not have been there on the pond. I feel it was God causing my mother to call out with a loud voice calling us at the right time, God saved us that day. God who is a very present help in the time of trouble. Thank God.

I also remember while living in that house my brother and I went scouting to an old abandon house looking to see what we could find, He heard a noise coming from under an old burlap bag on the porch. When he lifted the bag a swarm of bees attached him and he fell down and roll. I watched the horrid incident, he yelled for me to throw the bag over him. I was frozen and could not move. The bees stung him so bad his face swelled up (he looked like a monster to a little child). I was afraid of how he looked. His face stayed swollen for days. My mom nursed him back to health with old home remedies of snuff juice and tender loving care. This incident left me feeling guilty that I didn't do anything to help him. I didn't know what to do I was afraid of being stung myself.

Needless to say we were very adventurously children, my dad referred to us as Bertha's raiders whenever he was angry at us. We were always exploring and going and doing things some of what we were not suppose to be doing; mischievous but not destructive. In this small rural area in which we lived there were many snakes of all kind, poisonous and nonpoisonous and wild animals too, which made it dangerous for us. But God kept us and watched over us, I truly understand this now.

I remember my mom telling us about an incident that happened to her and my older brother on their way to a neighbor's house, Mr. George I believe it was, however they heard a cry that sounded like a baby crying, (there were a legend of how a panther would make sounds like a baby crying to lure his prey) that dust dark evening she told my brother not to make a sound just turn around and run, and they made it home safe. The next day some trackers supposed to have found tracks of a wild animal.

We made life exciting and with never a dull moment. We created games to play, things to do and created fun for ourselves outside the house, (something I feel now is long forgotten). New toys were rare for us so we made due for what we had. We collected old toys and tire rims and things from old junk piles to make play things for ourselves. We would use tin cans to make pretend walkies-talkies for ourselves. We used cans and strings to make tom walkers. We took pieces of tin from the old houses to used them for sliding down hills. We would swing on long vines across the lake pretending we were Tarzan and drop into the lake. We would go swimming in those big grudge ditches that were dug for irrigation, not too far from our house. They told me I was not allow to go in the water because I was too little.

My sister and I learned to make mud dolls and little villages and towns to play with. Money was scarce so during Christmas time mom and dad would concentrate on buying food, so new toys were very rare. I remember receiving a new little doll and my sister a big new doll with hair molded into the head and we kept those dolls forever it seemed. My mom would make doll clothes for them. My two brothers would receive cap pistols and they would play cowboy and Indians. Shooting the caps pistols in our ears as they sneaked up behind us to frighten us every chance they got.

When we moved from the haunted house we live in a house by the side of the road people called the four fork of the road. I still to this day don't know why it was called that: because the road was made like a "Y". We lived in this house until I was about 8. It was a two-bedroom house so all the children slept in a room together.

This house had cracks in the walls and ceilings we could look out to the sky and sometimes play imaginary game with the light that shown through. Sometimes my sister and I would put the covers over our heads and play with the light that shown through until we fell asleep. There were an old shed near the house, my sister and I asked if we could use it for a doll house so we set it up just like our real house and played for hours of the day in it.

I could remember a big portion of my time being spent alone, mom doing her house chores and the siblings off to school. I would leave the house and go looking for pecans, there were plenty of pecan trees around the area and there were a black walnut tree that stood on a hill which was a good distance from the house. I was always spooked to go there because I had to cross a church and a graveyard. But sometimes I would mustard up enough courage to go there and pick up black walnuts: they were my favorite.

As far as I could remember we always had some media entertainment. I remember sitting around the radio listening to daily stories being read. My mom's favorite gospel songs being played on the radio. The Family would sit together watching our favorite TV shows: such as the Long Ranger, Zero, Amos and Andy, Walt Disney, Kit Carson, Jim Bodie, Cheyenne, Daniel Boone, Mousekeeters, Roy Rogers, John Wayne (my mom's favorite), Ed Sullivan show, three stooges, Popeye the sailor-man, (my dad's favorite, he would always mark the Popeye song).

The Little Rascals show was my favorite. We enjoy good times watching television and listening to radio. But my greatest family time was when we gathered on the front porch to sing and tell stories and even during the winter when we would gather around the potbelly heater and eat my dad's popcorn.

Going to school was one of my favorite things to do. I enjoyed school so much. We all attended the St. Mary Elementary School. Where Mrs. Booker was the principle and teacher of 4th through 6th grade and Mrs. Alberta

Anderson was the k-3rd grades. It seems I quickly excelled through k-3rd and soon found myself in Mrs. Booker's classroom. I was the star of the class so I thought. I was smarter than any of the students and had to help other students even older than myself learn. My class was the last class to graduate before they closed the school. School was an adventure for me I was early every day and received an award for having a perfect attendance record. I received a 2 year subscription of the "Highlite Magazine". I would sometimes beat the janitor there and was so cold before a fire was started in the big black heater. Sometimes I would walk by myself to school, sometimes I would leave with my dad and it was so cold he would build a fire alone the road. Sometimes I would stop at some friends house and wait for them to get dress for school, just to have some one to walk with.

Then a boy named Darnell became my walking buddy. His grandmother told me to come by the house everyday to wake him up to get dressed for school. I was a shy kind of person but with a mean streak and very timid. My mom had always told us to never pick a fight but to always defend yourself. So that was me defending myself and others too. I remember once approaching a boy that had a brick in his hand. He was threatening to hit a friend of mine with it. I told him to put that brick down for he was not going to hit anybody with that brick. He told me that his mom told him to defend himself, I told him that she didn't mean to hit any one with a brick. He listened and put the brick down. I explained to him, that Gladys liked him and wanted to be his friend. As time went on everybody knew my name and who I was through out the whole school. I had my favorite buddy Gladys and others would follow. I could do anything but tell time. Later on a boy from my class named George taught me the concept and I began to understand, it seemed I caught on fast. Aah yes a star was born.

While it was certain that learning came easy for me. I still had my struggles of insecurity, shyness, vanity, selfishness, false pride, and the whole nine yards. My very first day of school the head teacher told me to go home and not come back without proof of being age six. I cry that whole day and could not wait until I got home to tell mom what had been said. The teacher didn't believe I was six years old and this reaction would follow me all my life in some form or another. People didn't believe how old I was to this day. So the next day my mom visited the school and got it all straighten out.

My first book to read was a primary reader. I told my brother I didn't want that book for it was too easy. He said throw it away then and I did just that. I got a first grade reader the next day and had been reading every since. I love to read. I remember my first reading lesson with my dad. He would spank me on the hand every time I say hat instead of cap. I will never forget that reading lesson. I believe it made me a better reader where I could teach others to read and I am still helping others to become better readers today.

We would walk to church if some one would not stop along the way to pick us up.

As I reflect back, one Sunday coming from church and we were picked up by a Mr. Bell, a family friend and he appeared to be taking us home but we stopped at a friends house along the way. Dee and I was told to stay with these friends. I didn't want to, I wanted to stay with mom, but she ordered me to get out of the car and stay with Dee. I refused to stay after I got out of the car and they drove off I started walking down the road toward home.

Dee asked me where I was going. I turned and said "home." She said mom told you to stay with me. I said no and kept walking. Dee got her boyfriend to come to try to take me back in his car but I ran across the field and stayed until they drove off. Then I came back to the house and stayed until night fall. I became frighten to be in the house all by myself, but finally C boy (my younger brother)came home around six o'clock that evening. I was very stubborn and silly I guess but was determined to be by myself if I could not stay with Mom. As I look back, I realize I was stubborn and wanted my way or nothing else mattered. I suppose I was pretty selfish. As I grew up I noticed that I was selfish and stubborn it followed me. I was not happy unless I was getting my way and that we were doing what I wanted to do or see happen even in school. After graduating from elementary school I went to Junior High school where I was on the honor role and was chosen runner up student of the whole school. I got to go upon stage in the school assembly. My name was put in the local news paper for writing a story. I went on the radio. All this was an exciting experience.

It was indeed "what about me and what I wanted" as Joyce Meyers would say. I feel now that God has showed me a lot of things over the years and I think that I have come into maturity some what. I like to think that I have grown both natural and spiritual. I can see clearly now as the fog has cleared and I learned over the years that it is not about me. I feel in my first marriage I tried to learn how to be less selfish and catered to my husband and the needs of the children while we were together. I tried to learn how not to put my feelings first. I took a lot from that marriage but learned the hard way. I took lots of bitter pills by way of lessons learned. Some how I feel I am the better for it and yet at the same time that chapter in my life hurts and I sometimes feel I played the fool. But isn't there a song that says you "Play the fool for love" and also "everybody plays the fool some times" however it is my hope that I learn from my mistakes.

During my marriage with Lewis, I allow 3 men to enter on a friendly manner. I enjoyed their attention since I was not really getting any from my husband. There were several men I could have gotten and played the adulterous field if I wanted too; like my husband was doing. Somehow deep down inside I knew what Lewis was doing but never wanted to admit it. I had people to come to me and say things about him and his relationship with other women. I suspected it before they even said. I had seen so much adulterous situations and overtures in my childhood so I was very aware of what might have been going on.

Women coming by the house calling out Lewis' name, in a sexual manner, long trips away from home, out all night coming in at 2 or 6 even 7 in the morning with excuses. He didn't want me to have company or talk to anybody outside. But indeed I wasn't truly innocent. I liked the attention I got from those three admirers. One would give me a ride to my art classes at the community center. One would take me to church, one I held secretly in my heart from high school as an admirer.

There were other admirers at a distance and I knew this too. So in my heart I guess I was never faithful to Lewis like I really should have been. This some how gave me consolation that I was not entirely fooled by Lewis' actions during our marriage. But this still made me vulnerable to the devils play. Because if our thoughts are not pure we are not pure and this could soon led to other things of actions. In the Bible scriptures tells us to think on whatsoever thing are pure holy, right,.and so as a man thinketh so is he.. A man looks upon a woman have committed adultery in his heart Phil.4:8, Mat.5:28, Proverbs 23:7).

Reflection even further I was sixteen. I went to a big City to stay with some family friends. A family of whom I had grown up with, that had left town. It was a chapter in my life I guess I won't forget. I knew Arthur Lee still liked me and I liked the attention. I had Lewis who was in the armed forces at this time. I was young and foolish. I gave into the attention and when I would get angry, I would mouth off and rant and rage. So finally I went to stay with my brother and his wife and there I stayed until I went home for that summer.

There were one incident that I won't forget that led up to my staying with my brother and his wife: it was when I stayed home from church one Sunday with Arthur Lee, his cousin Cast came over to the house. He and Arthur Lee began to tease and they got the best of me. I was outraged so I made up my mind to leave and stay with my brother this is how I came to stay with my brother. The mom and dad came home from church and my brother came too. I got even louder then and he asked what was going on, so I told my version of it and he said well go get your things. I had already formed a relationship with Gloria and her younger sisters, so she and I would see each other at the motel where we worked. I was glad to get away from that house.

That summer was an adventurous one for me. I saw my first mixed marriage. I worked my first major job, a real live maid for a motel. I experienced my first real adventure away from home. I felt I was my own person and I was really growing up. This experience also had another side to it. It was a terrible experience because I witness and learned of some of my oldest brother's woes with his wife. They would fuss and fight almost all the time. It was more sadness than happiness there. I had lots of mixed feelings growing up, and of course when I came home from that summer vacation. I told my Mom I would not have a man treating me poorly, she just looked at me.

When Lewis and I married of course he tried to treat me like a child and whip me. I hit bit and kicked and he got the message. He picked me up from school one day and saw me talking to a young man at the lockers and he formed an opinion and drove me down a dark road on pillow hill near the graveyard and there tried to whip me. I gave him a what for, after that he never tried that again. But he had the nerve to tell my Mom after we got home that I tried to kill him. Which was not true but I agreed with it because I was angry at him. Lewis and I fought once more when we were in Chicago this time it was my fault. I urged him on and I hit first but this time he only pushed me and kept pushing me down on the bed. Jack his brother, tried to break us up but I was too head strong. Lewis told me to stop before he hurt me and I stopped, all the time having a smile on his face. The fight was over with. We were fighting over another woman, something in which I told myself I would never do.

After this I never looked at Lewis the same way again. I lost something for him if I ever had something. Love I mean. I guess. But to be honest with you I think I lost the love passion for my husband when we had to leave our house and move back with our parents. He went to his mom? I moved back to my Mom. I later found out that he was living with the lady next door as husband and wife and when I confronted him I later learned that the child they had together died but I still stayed with him.

He left Arkansas going to Chicago, saying he would send for me and the baby later. Lewis sent just enough money to buy a ticket. I had a friend to help me get to Chicago, that friend gave me money enough to buy a big trunk and food for the trip. That summer in Chicago was a real life changing experience for all of us I guess. Lewis was out of work, he and Jack seems to never find work. They pretended to go out everyday looking for work but would manage to buy some liquor.

There were about 13 of us in one project 2 bed room apartment. I hated where we were. I hated our condition and the way they lived, I was not used to that.(There were some good things about it I guess. I met his Aunt Sugar, his brother Jerry and family, and saw my cousin Bertha while I was there.) I went looking for a job and found one in a hatbox factory. I worked until the end of the summer. I told my boss that my mom was sick and I needed to go home to Arkansas.

He gave my wages early. I left work, went to the apartment and packed my bags. I told Lewis that my baby and I was going home. I told Lewis he could come if he wanted too but I was leaving that day. We both moved back to Arkansas and moved into the house with his mom. That was a huge mistake. We were always at each others throat about something. After about a couple of weeks I moved into my mom's house and Lewis eventually came too.

Lewis found a job at the chemical plant and eventually we moved out into a project of our own. Times were hard we barely had food. I had one dress to wear and I seemed to be pregnant all the time. We would go back and forth to his mom and mine to eat. My mom provided clothes for the babies from a white lady she worked for. Thank God for Mothers!!!!

My Young Adult Life

I made a lot of dumb mistakes in my life, of which I am not proud of. Some I was able to make it right, others are long gone and so I asked God to forgive me so He placed them in the great sea of forgetfulness. So I move on hoping to never to repeat those mistakes again. I realize now that trial and tribulations comes to make us strong.

Hopefully more dependent on God's guidance and directions. But sin is not without consequences, we must pay for the deeds done in the body. Hopefully a little wiser and to lean and depend on God. While we are here on this earth God gives us a second chance to do an about face.

I got married at the age of 18, while in High School in Arkansas. I was pregnant the marriage lasted 3 years. They were the most unhappy years of my life. They were worst than being sickly all my life. I left town, the marriage, and my husband after our 3rd child was born. She was only 1 months. I moved to St. Paul, in September 21,1973.

I conceived 3 wonderful children out of this union they I don't regret. Lewis, my marriage on the other hand is another matter. I later learned that he had two other children nearly the same age as mine.

I joined and attached myself to a church called Shiloh. The following Sunday after our arrival, because my mom had told me earlier to do so as quick as possible. I enjoyed the services and the preaching. But I hated the people's teasing and pounding and taunting me about how young I was. Making statements about how I was too young to have all those babies. I was just a baby myself. So I allowed the enemy to cheat me out of quitting the church for a whole year. I started to have bible study in my home with an Jehovah witness. She would come every week. I liked that because I would not have to take the children out in the winter cold. I studied all winter with her. In the spring I moved and lost track of her after attending her Kingdom Hall once. I was not sad about losing track of her especially after her telling me, that the world would come to an end in 1977. However I felt God had His hand on me even then.

I met a new man in my life: a man whom, I thought loved me and my children and wanted to marry me. He and I dated for almost a year. I was mistaken, but was already pregnant. I considered abortion. My conscience got the best of me and especially when my doctor told me they did not do abortion there, that I could go down to the Ramsey hospital. After giving birth, I was told it was a boy, I was so thankful that I did not abort him. I thought I would never have a boy after having three girls prior.

Later in July 1974 a new man came into our lives: the children (my three girls) loved him and called him "their Alboo". Albert fell in love with the baby as if it was his own. I became jealous, secretly. I knew Albert from childhood. His sister (she and I became good friend after my moving to the big city) had told me earlier that he had always liked (had a crush on) me in grade school.

Good times seems to be happening and we were happy, it seemed. I had my baby and Albert asked me to be his girlfriend that summer. My children and I moved to the suburbs of St. Paul to the McDonald projects in the fall of that year. He moved in with us in the suburbs during the winter of 74. After moving to the suburbs, I took up driving school, softball, community projects, cooking and sewing and helping out the head-start school program.

Needless to say I was not attending church during this period of time. I would send my children to a church near us because the people would come and get them on a bus. I attended a couple of times myself but never joined. I remember it was a fall of '76 and I had finished hanging my clothes on the outside line and the telephone ranged: when I answered; it was to my surprise that my pastor of Shiloh was on the other end. He stated "we are having a revival at the church and was wondering if you was planning on attending." I said yes before I knew it, still amazed from the pastor calling me of all people!, so when the time came I went, the very first night I rededicated my life back to God, and I been on the active role every since. I appreciated and took my second chance. We were still living in the suburbs of the city during this time(I had to ride the bus back in town) and later moved back in the heart of the Big city, what the children called the hood. On Western street.

The children had already falling in love with their Alboo and he was good to us, but when he asked me to marry him, my first answer was no at first. I was so mixed up in the head and afraid after all the mistakes I had already made that I was going to make another, but soon after I said yes. We were married in June 11, 1976 after our son was born, in December 13, 1975.

I spent my honeymoon in church. (Prior to our marriage my pastor wanted Albert and I to come for counseling but Albert refused so I went alone. I must explain that Albert had asked Rev. Eli to perform the wedding but my pastor said no and that He should do it himself, Albert did not know the pastor of Shiloh). I remember my pastor stating "Sis. Arnett a newly wed is here today instead of being on her honeymoon she was married on yesterday". The congregation laughed.

But I have to tell you my decision did not come without consequences, my husband did not come with me in my new found life with God, in fact, Two years later we began to have problems. My new husband and I went to Arkansas with the family in 1977 for a summer vacation. Shortly after that I took a job at Kmart, (he did not want me to work,) but I went any ways. I was determined to have my own money.

I told myself I wanted my own money and I hated asking my husband for what I wanted and needed, (a trick of the enemy). We soon separated in the fall of 1979 when I got home from work I found a letter from my husband stating "he did not want to be a husband and a father anymore". We were off and on the whole time about 6 times in our separation periods. The last time I was calling it quit. I was making plans to leave town, in 1984 headed to the Big city, where my mom had moved.

I was making plans and seeking employment through the city newspapers. I had a friend who was helping me by sending me newspapers and updates of job and housing possibilities. I told no one from the church of what had happened nor of my planning to move until much later, I was too embarrassed. So with work and softball and school and the children we pushed ahead as best we could for about 6 months. My activities never stopped, my routine never changed; except for trying to find a baby sitter from time to time. My children and I drove down to Rochester, for a change of pace and a light weekend vacation.

I came from work one day, I had been fasting and praying and still going to church. I finally has a conversation with my pastor after a crying spell that did not want to stop. I sought some advise with a Deacon at church, whom I observed as a father figure in my life for consolation. I told my girl friend Bonita at work but by then, I had made up my mind to leave town. My husband would drop by, from time to time and one day he came by to tell me he wanted his family back, that he missed his family. Why now in the midst of my plans? I was mad and I didn't want to accept him back.

I was getting my life together and moving on so I thought. I had this uncontrollable crying spell to come over me at work one day, so I called my pastor. He and I talked over the phone and I told him, that my husband and I had been separated for 6 months. He repeated it in unbelief and said but you never stop coming to church. I told him I felt I could handle it and that I was strong to handle every thing in my life this was the reason I never let on, I never stopped going to church, I never stop participating in events, in fact I was nominated runner up mother of the year. I felt this was too private and I was raised that what ever went on in the family stays in the family no outsider had to know or should know.

My Steps into Maturity

One day as I was parking the car from work, I heard the Holy Spirit speak to me, "not this one", I said Lord he left us. I don't know if I want him back. I believed the Heavenly Father was telling me that He had released me from my first marriage, but not this one, not this time. I must stay and make it right. So I obeyed and my husband and I got back together, but of course not without consequences, I wanted revenge I guess. I had been hurt, trampled on and now I am to take him back!

It seems like all hell broke loose instead of living happy ever after it was kiosk, arguments, a lot of unanswered questions because my husband was calling it the past and didn't want to talk about it. I felt I was hurting and he didn't want or didn't know how to heal my pain so he kept saying I don't want to talk about it. That wasn't the answer I wanted to hear. I felt not talking was making it worse. We could never see eye to eye, and never agreed on any thing. I was miserable, so I sought out counsel. But of course my husband was oblivious to why we were seeking counseling. He felt all was hunky dory, so when we came for counseling he didn't know what was going on and why we were there.

I had questions about the other woman, and of course there were phone calls from the other woman. Who at one point cursed me out over the telephone, but she died tragically and as time went on and things settled. I truly gave our marriage to God, God began to heal our marriage. God shut my mouth while I was learning to be still and quiet before Him. I began to grow in God.

The children's Alboo started going to church and I slowly left Shiloh in 1985. Where I had become every office position in the church except secretary to the pastor. I joined my husband at the Faith Deliverance Church, which I believed changed both our lives. I believed that God had drawn me there. I now understand that this is the way I had to go in order for God to get my attention that he was calling me to be a preacher. I believe I had mentioned it all ready that God anointed me in my bedroom while I was in bed a bright light filled the whole room and I was frighten. I thought I was going to die.

I asked if I was dying and the presence said "lie still I am anointing you", so he did anoint me from the feet to the head three times and he left. I thought how strange it was that I could not awake my husband he was as if he was dead to the world. As I nudged him he would not move so the presence said lie still.

For the period 1985 to 1994 we enjoyed going to church together, the whole family was going together, first Bold Gospel where my husband first became a deacon. Then the Living Word. The children was growing up. I heeded God's calling on my life and finally excepted in 1987 and was licensed in 1988. But you see I asked God when had he first called me and he stated in 1985. I know now that I had to be in a position of receiving. Because I was in a church that did not believe in Women preachers. I was in agreement of this thought pattern also.

My husband was a deacon we had prayer in our home, bible study and worship and praise service. I enjoyed learning about the Holy Spirit, having a prayer life and a prayer partner. I began to speak in other languages. I was ordained in 1996 by Rev Carl Walker. We will never have these Bible studies again. We attended 3 churches during the process of God using me to be his instrument of ministry. I believed God told me to come out of the church called The Living Word Church and go back into the baptist setting in 1994. Once again my husband and I was separated, only this time spiritually. He did not want to leave the church where we was currently attending. I knew God had closed the doors to me, so he stayed for a little while at the old church.

I attended church at the baptist setting, and my husband soon stop going all together. By this time the children was all teenagers and making their own decisions.

We had bought a home in Woodbury suburbs in 1991. Our two teenage boys still in high school. My husband and I had decent jobs. But in 1992 I got laid off from my University job. I went to work for the Penumbra theater for just a short winter season.

Then in 1993 I worked as secretary and accounting clerk for our church, later to Walker West Studio. I was fired after becoming ill in 1995. Later finding jobs here and there working with Account Temps.

After becoming ill and then laid off again in about 1996. I applied and took a job in training with the HealthEast Hospital system as a chaplain until 1998. I later landed a Interim Chaplain position in the Regency

Hospital until 1999. Later working again with Account Temps but by this time, my husband had the business fever. He quit his steady job and went to work for himself and later a local cleaning company and some bad deals and bad decisions was made. We got behind in our mortgage.

I was called in the fall of 1999 to work as a full time Chaplain for the HealthEast System until 2001. In 2000 my 5 year old grandchild died needless to say it was a terrible blow to my entire being and in 2002 my Mother died. Now I felt I was loosing my mind. Truly it was God's amazing grace that brought me through it all. His grace was truly precious as it appeared to me. God had a earthly angel and a plan for my life, so He kept me and brought me through and healed both mind and body. Let me interject.(I must say in 2003 I traveled to a Revival in Mississippi with my prayer partner I was sick then. But I had heard from the Holy Spirit that I should not allow my illness to hinder my going (because prior to that trip I had been turning down every invitation I had received.)

While on the trip God interjected some things in my spirit and when I returned I was soon healed. I was visited by my Mother while lying on the sofa in pain and shortly after the visit I fell asleep. I didn't even realize the pain was gone and the swelling went down in my foot after I had awaken.

Then went back to work for the Account Temps and by 2003 fell sick again and lost that job. After making one bad decision after another concerning our finances. I felt I was not giving my husband enough support went along with some bad decisions and finally we lost the house. So in 2007 we moved into a rather nice rental house, there we stayed for about 2 years, later moving into an apartment building as Caretakers of that building by the suggestions of his sister in 2009. But through all of this I asked God to please help me not to become angry and bitter toward my husband for all that had happened. My husband refers to all what has happened to us as our decisions, so there you have it. We are in this together. Until death do us part. I must say God gave me strength to move on and through it all we lack nothing that was vital, health, food, clothing and a roof over our heads.

Life goes on: I believe God sees us through all the mistakes, the pain, some of our own bad choices in life, some that are not, but God see us through it all. When we fall, God then gives us strength to bare it and rise up again. God is our very present help in time of need. After all, His word does tell us that He will never leave or forsake us. I felt God finally healed our marriage and made our love for each other stronger than ever. After I let go and latched on the Him. I am truly not perfect or have arrived but I believe it's fair to say I have made a major milestone in my life. Of course we never stop growing spiritually, until we die. It is called coming into maturity.

I feel my life have taken a turn for the better as I mature. God have revealed a great many things to me. I have traveled a many places and accomplished many things in my life. I have learned to let go of old wounds and hurts and the past that so easy beset me. I now press toward the mark of the prize of the higher calling that God has placed on my life. Even that has it's obstacles, but I know I must lean and depend on God's help.

I tend to hold on to things, peoples. Trying to reach out to them even after they are gone and still find myself wanting. I am learning that people come and go in your life and at some point I had/ have to let go. (It's as if God has somehow let go and I know I must also.)

God has closed that chapter in my life or it has ran it's course or served it's purpose. It's called transitioning: where God turns you and twists you and molds you into what He would have you to be: realizing that He will be turning and twisting and molding until you die.

I remember I heard the Holy Spirit tell me to not to become content or stagmented in what ever I am doing for HIM. I now understand that He will move me on. So I must be flexible and pray constantly and seek His face for direction. I realize that others might not understand me, but that should not deter me. I must obey GOD. I must obey God. Peter speaks of this in the New Testament writings (Acts 5:29).

I view my spiritual life as having phases. As I write this I think hard on this: These phases are:

<u>Phase I</u>: Childhood: where God basically held my hand all the way as I took baby steps along my faith walk. I left but God called me out of the church of almost 14 years. I have mentioned the experience early on in the book. Accepting that I had to leave, all my friends and church family that I had made. I was trying hard not to be disobedient. The Holy Spirit building me up to the right time to tell the pastor. God worked that out so smoothly. By giving the perfect time and atmosphere in which to sit down with my pastor and my husband.

<u>Phase II:</u> Adolescent I understand why they call it adolescent because for me it was my trying time, My finding the edge or the grip on my spiritual journey and my adulthood or maturity: I learned all about the working of the Holy Spirit: How He is walking on the earth today

and working in us to do God's will. I heard God's voice that I was his hand and feet extended.

<u>Phase III:</u> I hesitate when I write the word maturity because I feel that I will be forever coming in to maturity. Paul refers to it as moving from milk to meat but did not tell us when that meat stage would end. But when I recognized the Holy Spirit's presence, speaking in tongues (other languages), dancing in the spirit. Hearing God speak to my spirit man, my mind: I believe there were some mature growth.

I was up speaking once and the Holy Father I believe instructed me to give reference to or acknowledge the Holy Spirit presence. Most people believe that the Holy Spirit is an it. But He is indeed a person. Otherwise why would GOD ever tell me to give reference to Him before all those people if He weren't a real person. It's not that I did not know the Holy Spirit but I believe it was for someone's benefit. Who ever it was in the audience that was struggling with that issue at that time.

An Eye Opening Step

I mentioned earlier that my spiritual journey has phases, well these phases has steps. <u>Step 1:</u> I stepped into my calling that God had placed on my life: I stepped into my awareness that He had called a woman (Me). The next was acceptance of the anointing that faithful night of the visit in my bed room. Getting past the fear of rejection of my calling. The acknowledging of my calling. For God told me I had to tell people. Receiving the Five-fold ministry gifts that God had given me. I went around asking people if they believed that God would give someone the five-fold ministry to one person namely me. Looking for people to confirm me.

Step 2: Coming into the awareness of being a Bishop without knowing what it really was until years later. Being called a priest by God and being anointed by God's messenger to teach the Gospel. Coming into the awareness of the five-fold ministry gifts and the anointing of being an intercessory and Prayer warrior.

Step3: Looking for man's approval of me and God had told me several times that it was just Him and me. He wanted to train and teach me; Telling me that I was an watchman on the wall early in my ministry calling. Teaching me from His perspectives.

Step 4: Being licensed twice by two separate non-denominational ministries, and later being ordained from a Baptist Perspective.

Step 5: Educating myself and walking in the ministry gifts that God has placed in my life. Training and Learning to become a spiritual chaplain while I worked in the hospitals, and the prisons. I believe I truly heard God's voice speaking to me with clarity. "I am thine Ol' Lord I have heard thine voice and it had told me what to do". I believe my life is fuller and I am more happier than I had ever been in my life.

An Awareness of Brotherly Love and Reconciliation:

In 2001 I joined a Unification Movement (after having a Japanese Missionary and a Black pastor visit my church as we were worshiping) called American Clergy Leadership Conference those of us affectionately refer to as ACLC. Since my connecting with this movement I have travel extensively in the USA and a broad having traveled prior to my joining makes a grand total of about 40 states. I traveled to Israel on a Peace Mission, by way of Rome, Italy in 2003. I travel to China on an Ambassador for

Peace Conference in 2005, traveled to Japan and Korea to establish the Choen IL Guk and Peace Mission in October 2006 and later this year 2011 traveled back to Korea to establish Sisterhood among our Korean brothers and sisters in September. During my visit there I was able to attend the world's largest church. I also watched the unveiling of a shine which was a symbol of the four great religious leaders of the world. I am realizing that God is establishing the evangelism in me of the Five-Fold ministry gifts that He has bestowed upon me back in 1987 when he first called me into the ministry.

As I discipline myself to be obedient to God. I heard Him tell me to let the church be swallowed up by the Unification Church, It was hard but I obeyed. I closed the doors in 2007. I sold most and gave some of the things that was in the building to other ministries. I feel there were a sense of freedom attached to what I had done.

Through extensive research, reading and praying and meditating I have some insights that has caused me to grow. I thank God for my life so far and my life in general, although I am not total happy for all the crooks and turns that came in my life, during the time I strayed away, but I am thankful to God who caused me to find my way back to Him. I found Him standing there with outstretched arms ushering me near to Him.

Through all my growing pains (some of us have to learn the hard way) God is molding and shaping me into what He would have me to be. You see: God is still molding and shaping because I am still in my maturity phase of life.

The Mercies of God Revealed

My life could have been a disaster, but God made some good come out of it all. God is the head of my life now and I want to follow His leading and guiding all the way. I have learned to seek ye first the kingdom and God's righteousness and all will be added. I have learned to lean not to my own understanding, I have learned to ask, seek and knock of God and He never leaves nor forsake, and a very present help in the time of need. God has always been with me even when I turn my back on him those trying times in my life. He never turned his back on me, I have learned over the years that our actions have consequences and our life is not our own, so when we commit acts of sin, we hurt a lot of people and God not just ourselves.

After learning this I made a conscience effort to say Lord help me bring no shame to your name in thought word or deed. As I walk this journey I have learned I will never walk alone. There is a old song "Lord Guide my feet while I run this race" this is my motto. There are two scriptures which are near and dear to my heart, "I have hidden thy word in my heart that I might sin against thee, and thy word is a lamp unto my feet and a light unto my past way" (Psalms 119:11 & 119:105).

My five children and my husband are now very near and dear to my heart, because I have learned over the years that it is not about me but God and through this life lesson: I learned to live for the sake of others. I have learned that my children was a gift from God and that he had lone them to me to see if I could help mold and shape them into His image. If I would teach them the values of GOD. If I would take on the responsibility of raising them in the admonition of His love and goodness. In other words train up the children. I have learned that my family is my church and that through Rev Sun Myung Moon teachings that we are indeed one family under God. So I asked myself what is it to go to heaven with out your family??? In fact we might not make it without them. I believe God places people in your life in order that you might learn and grow from them and the experiences are there to make you ever to depend on him at all times. Not that you should not stand on your own two feet but that knowing God, you can and will stand strong on your own two feet.

The Lord gave me the name for the church I was to call it "The Mercies of God". It was early one morning as I lie in bed I was visited by a happy messenger, a big smile and bouncing around and saying I know the name of your church: and I said you do "what is it" and He told me. It was years later that I put it on paper and registered it with the state as an established entity, but there it was finally, at last. I stepped out on faith for almost 10 years it would last. I was semi-encouraged by my husband who kept telling me that I was afraid to step out. It was though prayer that I kept hearing God's voice, but I kept working with the prison ministry and with the Morning Star church as if there were no calling on my life to establish a church.

While I was there at the Morning Star for 4 years. I sought out another voice and had a conference with a Pastor Harold Echol in Minneapolis who said yes it is time to start. I finally made up my mind to talk with my own pastor. I also told him I was not there to take any members of his church that I was sent there to help his ministry and I felt that I had done my part and the God was calling me out to established my own. He agreed and stated that I would make a fine pastor and he gave me his blessings. I thanked him and I left. I was ordained in 1996 and two years later I started the church. The Lord had told me earlier that it was not a traditional church but I kept trying to make it out of one.

The Lord had called this church an opened door church with a street ministry. All the while I was try to witness to bring sheep into the fold the more I witness the less people attended. It appeared to grow but it will become stagmented so much so that an outsider looking in pulled me to the side and told me that I should have been zooming by now and that I needed a spiritual father to cover me. I allowed this person to ordain me as his spiritual daughter, but that soon fell by the waste side. I was told that very night of the ordaining service I received a prophecy "that people had been telling me that I had stepped out to early and that I should have been farther alone but God said not so I have you just where I want you; your ministry is a hard one but you are to hold on and let God do it. I screamed and fell to the floor, because the weight of their voices were heavy on my mind and heart. But it all boiled out of jealousy and envy. God gave me a relief.

Even after the prophecy my prayer partner asked me if I had step out and should not have been. My point is that I knew I heard from God that should have been enough: but

I allowed other voices to cloud my thinking and hearing and obeying. I listened to man. Instead of my hearing my Pastor friend who was telling me: "not to receive these voices because I was the pastor. I was the one God had called and that I should hear him and be steadfast". I finally pulled aside and started to end the friendship with my prayer partner because she was being influenced by another women in her church who had a jealous spirit on her regarding me, because she had lost her church and I still had mind. This is a clear case of leaning not to you own understanding but in all your ways acknowledge God. I thought I was doing that but it was clearly that I was not.

I went to a prayer conference retreat that same year and I received a prophecy that people who had influence in my life was not my friends. I needed to hear from God. I got whipped by trying to listen to man's advice instead of just obeying God. We need to obey God no matter what people think. Everybody has something to say but their opinion is not worth any thing we must obey God. I took unnecessary chastisement and all I needed to do is hear from God and obey Him. Scripture reference Obedience is better than sacrifice. I Samuel 15:22. I learned a lesson that my Mom use to say "You cannot tell everybody your receiving from God. Everybody don't need to know. It use to be put like this "don't let the right hand know what the left hand is doing".

There are levels of growth that God takes us through, some call it growing pains, but it can be as painful as you make it, but if you learn how to let go then with the pain God will strengthen you for the growth. While God is stretching us, we can look back and wonder if there were not a God carrying us through all of it. How would we have stood the storms?

In 2007 God placed a man in my life that would changed the way I looked at myself for all times. God caused Bishop Charlie Robinson to ordained me as Bishop. Now I must tell you that God called me bishop back in 1991 but at that time I knew not what a bishop was or did so I placed it on the back burner of my mind.

I must tell you that prior to that God had already asked me did I want to know what the Lazarus in the Bible job was. I must confess I did not know what God was doing. So I asked Him why would I want to know what Lazarus job was? But now I understand that God was trying to give me a heads up prior to this ordaining in my life. God was setting me up and getting me ready. I wonder do you know that God shows us the outcome before He shows us the happening. In other words, He tries to mold and shape us to fit the job and purpose that He has for us. God is preparing us to accomplish the work He has ordained for our lives. Only He knows when we are ready. All he wants us to do is be willing. (Lazarus was a Bishop of Kittium.)

After all, our trials comes to make us strong, strong in our faith, strong in our belief, and strong to lean and depend on God. Life is a spiritual batter, a spiritual warfare, and we are victorious in the life with God because the battle has already been won; we need not fight in this battle just believe in God. Because we are more than conquerors through Him.

Over the years I have seen relentless times that God has intervened in my life, tearing down strong holds, uplift spirits, moving obstacles, shaping lives, using me for His glory, fighting countless battles, and showing me the way out of what I thought was no way. I have truly found that with God nothing is impossible. He took a small county girl from the back woods of Arkansas and brought her to a great place called Minnesota and gave me countless people whom I can call friends. God established my feet on solid grounds with Him. God has given me the blessed assurance that He is with me all the way if I walk with Him, abide in Him. For He is the Vine and I am the branch. I have made a decision to follow Jesus all the rest of my life, all the days of my life. In my following Jesus, I had to establish a relationship with Him because I felt that was the only way, I would assure my self that I knew Him and He truly knew me.

I belonged to God through Jesus' blood covering. I understand that plainly. I learned at an early age that Jesus was the only way. That was my belief that was my faith walk. That was my teaching and has now become my life. I have learned to be tolerable to other religions because I love people and the scripture tells us to love one another it did not base that love on that person's religion, and of course I could win more bees with kindness that I could anything else.

There is a scripture that said "love and kindness have I drawn thee (Jeremiah 31.3), so I took on that mind set. I believe scripture that stated Those who win souls must be wise. And of course wisdom comes from God (Proverbs 2:6). So I wanted to please God so that I could receive wisdom. Because scripture states if one lacks wisdom let him ask of God for it pleases him to give. (Ecclesiastes 2:6). Needless to say that I began asking. I took the scripture of Proverbs as my own: "that states get wisdom get knowledge and all thy getting get understanding" (Proverbs.4:4-7). So until I understood God's ways for my living I asked day and night. Because 2 Chronicles 7:14 states "Humble yourself, and pray, seek his face, and turn from your wicked ways, then He would hear from heaven and heal your land". I understood there was something that I must do for it was a command that came from God. I made it a personal challenge. For I truly believed that with God on my side I could do all things because He was strengthening me to do the task (Phil. 4:13).

As I began to study and search and truly seek God in His Word and educate myself with the spiritual things. I felt God. I knew God. I heard Him speak to me more and more. And when He became silent I learned that I must be still to hear what he was saying to me. I would dream dreams, hear words, phrases and sentences. I received unctions and therefore became very confident that God was using me in prayer, in scripture and deeds. I was a teacher, pastor, evangelist I began to understand some things. I was searching after God's own heart. I was striving to be the ideal Christian that God wanted me to be. When God told me I was on the right track I could stick my chest out and say, yes God I hear and obey. I strive to be that Idea child of God.

There are higher heights and deeper depths in God and every round truly goes higher and higher. There are always learning stages in our life and we will always be learning until we die. God showed me a ladder that was straight from earth to heaven which indicated that as I climbed that ladder: It would take me higher and closer in Him.

In my early learning stages of spiritual adulthood, I heard the Holy Spirit say to me "That I was His hand and feet extended. As I began to grow spiritually mature I began to see and understand that we are Gods' hands and feet extended for He was not coming down here to help people physically any more but would reach people through us. So therefore we were to love people as we love ourselves and reach out to them because love is an action word. (James1:22).

I thought on the prophecy that was told to me a long while ago regarding: I was to see the world through Gods' eye. I began to see people whom I had never met before in the spirit realm, people far away and even near. God telling me to pray for them and lift them up to Him. I began to have love and compassion for them even empathy. I began to understand that I was a prayer warrior and an intercessory. I now understand that God has called all of us to be intercessors. We are to pray for one another. James 5:6 and many other scriptures.

So I became curious as to others thought patterns regarding prayer and intercessory. I was fortunate because God had already given me a pray partner, mature enough to know that prayer was much needed and that we could pray constant. So we began calling each other daily, night and day and reading scriptures. Coming together and lying out before God regularly. I began to grow spiritually more and more. I would witness on the streets, handing out pamphlets and taking names and praying for the people that God would open up their eyes.

Before I started chaplain school I got the unction to write an autobiography of myself. I wanted to tell of the events and challenges and experiences that I had encountered during my life and to see and look back where God brought me from. Through sickness in my childhood up to adult hood. My near death experiences and to just show how God has always been there with me and my very presence help in time of all my troubles, doubts and fears. There is a song of old that states: "I may have doubts and fears My eyes may fill with tears but Jesus is the one who watches day and night, I go to him in prayer He knows my every care".......

The life journey: Adulthood

In 1985 life as a true Christian really began I say this even though all my life I have been with Jesus. Even though I confess Jesus at the age of 12 to the public, I believed that in my heart and mind I knew Him. He walked with me, talked with me, showed me things in dreams and visions but I did not understand. I would read the Bible at a very tender age and imagined myself being right there with those people and their stories and the land. I look back over my life and say yes Lord I know you were with me, just like you told me. So here I am today walking as close with the Lord as I know how and seeking HIM for an even closer walk.

Psalms 23 summed my life up quite well as I walked on this journey. I wish I had a better understanding back then that I have now. Maybe I would not have made so many mistakes. Me make mistakes? While I am appalled. Yes me, no matter how close I tried to walk, I am human. I am going to make mistakes, stumble and fall but I get back up again. In my falling seven time I know God is with me (Proverbs 24:16). You must understand It's like Paul stated "When I try to do good evil is always presence" (Romans 7:21). This let's us know that we can't do it in our own strength: We need God's strength, wisdom and understanding.

God is a God of a second chance and chances and chances, until you get it right. God is long-suffering. He waits on us to get it right, with his tender mercies and his gracious goodness hovering over us continuously. I have an ugly past. One I would like to erase and pretend it never happened but if you don't go through something, you won't ever know if God can deliver/comforts you out of it (I Corinth 1:4). A lot of things I did not do, but it still did not make me righteous. I had to accept God as my savior and deliverer and allow HIM to clean me up. (John 3:16). For all have sinned and falling short of the Glory of God" (Romans 3:23).

When I asked God when did He call me into the ministry, He stated 1985. But you see I did not acknowledge it until 1988. When I understood the He was really nudging on me, preparing me, getting me ready. This I believe is why the bible states: "in all thy getting get an understanding." (Prov.4:7), because I did not believe in women preachers and all my life surrounded by this ignorance and belief that there were no women preachers and that God hadn't called women to be preachers and therefore you must understand: That what you don't know truly will hurt you, where as I had been hearing the opposite. I was attached to a church that was telling the people the same idea. No women preachers, and that they were never welcomed in his pulpit.

The enemy wanted to keep me ignorant and (anybody else who would listen to him,) thereby never entering into the calling that is upon my life. But my diligently seeking God, wanting more of Him, asking more of Him paid off.

God brought me into the calling that was upon my life and through prayer and fasting gave me a prayer partner(one in whom I kept asking for a friend) for almost 30 years. I have learned over the years don't put God in a box, or even place Him on a shelf until you are ready for

HIM. God demands us to spend time with Him if we want to come up higher and having a closer walk. This I think is why the Bible states" Man should always pray and not faint". and "Pray without ceasing."(I Thes.5:17 & Luke 18:1).

I prayed that God would help me to help myself: Can I do anything without you Lord. I have a hope within me and that hope is in you. Thank you for all you do to strengthen me and show me your way. A prayer in Colossians chapter 1 verses 9- 17 is a good one. This passage teaches us not to be selfish even in our praying. We should pray for wisdom. Wisdom comes from God to help us understand when we pray Proverbs 4:7 and Proverbs 2:6.

God had to deal with my inferiority complex. I had the complex that all whites were better than I was. And attached to that was the idea that everybody knew better than me, to the point that when even someone knew something I didn't know I would beat myself up with the thoughts that I should have known that. I was embarrassed by not knowing or even getting an answer wrong in school. So this inferiority complex had other strongholds, where the enemy got in and attached itself to my spirit. I was delivered by prayer, reading the Bible, fasting over the years. Seeking God's thought patterns about my life. Reminding myself to seek ye first the king and His righteousness and all else would be added constantly (Matthew 6:33).

Once while reading a book called "Are Blacks Spiritually inferior to Whites." I began to think of my life at that time. I was pushing the thought patterns (every chance I got) regarding the HUMAN RACE not Color orientated Race. I wondered within myself if I wasn't pushing the concept because of my own hidden fears of inferiority: that somehow my fears that I am unequal to Whites does indeed steer up out of my ignoring my true feelings that my fight is more than to tear down jealousy, hatred and strife among the human race but to tear down my fears of facing my thought patterns of some how feeling inferior. But as I contend with my faith I see and believe that I understand if it is a fear it's of the fact that I am inferior to them by God's standards not mans'. In other words: I am truly not inferior at all; but they do not measure up to me in any way.

For what God has placed within me is unique and no one can take that away because it came from God. (Psalm 139:19). I'm my own person inferior to no one but God: because God is my creator.(Roman:1: 25) and Deut. 28:13). Sometimes I wonder about my own self and think God has placed me above my siblings, using the Joseph, Manasseh and Ephraim situation in my family. (Gen.48:12-21.)

God visited me in my dream one night and awaken me with the phrase Ephraim I love, Manasseh I hate. I didn't understand it then I thought God wanted me to read the incident in the Bible perhaps make a sermon out of it or something. I don't think I am better than my siblings in any way it just that God's hand was steady upon me a little more than my siblings.

God guided my foot steps a little closer than the others perhaps. I understand it a little better now as I reflect on my life and the life of my siblings. Surely God is blessings them too. My life I accredited all to prayer and seeking God on a regular bases for all I have done; It's all to the glory of God.

In 1992 I became ill I was placed in the hospital, after coming back from my grandfather's funeral in Arkansas. I was taking to the hospital emergency room in Kansas city while attempting to take my mother home. The hospital told me that it might have been from the stress of the funeral and the trip. After returning home I went into the hospital. During my stay in the hospital; I had just arrived, they place me in a double occupant. The curtain was drawn between us and as I turned to lay comfortable I saw a presence that light up the room. He was dressed in a white suit, a very tall and handsome man with a big smile upon his face. I adjusted my eyes to get a good look. As I focused he was looking down at me smiling. He stated that He came to put the worse case of anxiety upon me I ever had. I stated I know who you are I rebuke you in the name of Jesus. The presence quickly vanished.

The doctors never found what was ailing me. After a weeks worth of tests, I was discharged for home. While I was there in the hospital my prayer partner and I prayed night and day for the pain to subside. She asked me did they give me pain medicines. I don't remember my response. But prayer helped better than anything else. After a long while praying even after being discharged from the hospital, I remember hearing a voice stating: "That's enough" and I don't remember when the pain ended.

As an adult I experienced God's hand around me leading me and guiding me as I prayed, sought after his guidance and leadership. I begin to listen, He took me through the establishment of the church the step by step process. The church purpose, the church doctrine, the church guidance, the church cleansing reading was all scriptures that came from Him. The church symbol, the model scripture as I began to implement them into the church worship service. I watched God as he spoke His words into my ears. I listened as carefully as I could. I saw how we as a people began to grow spiritually. Having confidence that whatever need there was God would take care of it. God stating that it was not a traditional church and that the ministry was hard and He was the one that was orchestrating it. He kept telling me that the church was in the street and that "Souls at any Cost" was my motto: The song kept guiding me as words "I am thine O Lord and I have heard thine voice it told me what to do" ringed over and over in my ears. Yet all I could see was that it was a traditional church because all I could see around was tradition, no one else was doing it: the way He was showing me.

God and I would have a talk morning evening or night, He visited me in dreams. Visions, and through people's mouths as confirmations. Day or night I would hear something that he had spoken to me or whispered to my spirit as confirmations. I became sick in church service and a preacher friend asked me if God had told me something and I wasn't doing it, this was before I actually stepped out on the call that God had placed in my life. I said to the preacher I was not sure that I didn't think so. But I knew that it meant I had to go back to my prayer closet and inquire of God.

In 1996 I began to study as a chaplain and went through the HealthEast Hospital system in order to train. That was a very interesting journey. As a chaplain in training I had the hands on approach and adopted very well and quickly right after I stopped crying. They took the student counseling approach and we had to stop by the instructors office and have a chat, now for me I thought this was a bunch of hog wash because I had never experienced anything such as this and for a black going to a white man was never heard of in my book of life.

So needless to say the first session of the schooling I had nothing to say and was evaluated as not using my personal time wisely. So the next session I began to open up, I prayed more listened to God more and talked during my training sessions about my experience as a chaplain on the patient floors and began to sit with the patients in their moment and listened to their stories. I learned many things but the two things that I really learned was that: I could sit with someone in their moment and did not have to give them an answer all I had to do is stop and listen and number two no matter what anybody else said or did, I was to hold on to what God had given me. Because no one could ever take that away but me.

So I listened carefully to the instructor and the other trainees and began to hear their stories which was in some cases very unique from mine. I was a recent graduate, had started to write my life story and very new to that kind of environment. Needless to say that I was the first black to ever venture with the HealthEast Hospitals and paved the way for many others to come their way. Being a chaplain in training and eventually a chaplain at work in an all white neighbor was a learning experience indeed, this experience took 4 years of my life. I am the better for it and could tell you the learning experience was well worth the journey and I would advise and suggest to many one to take the journey too, for they will never regret it.

After the training they ask you what you want to be when you grow up? I told them I was going to try my hand in pastoring: all of the trainees agreed that I would do well in this field because they believed it was my calling. I agreed also because I knew it was God's calling upon my life. You see God had already told me and I believe He was preparing me for the journey years earlier. When

I preached my first sermon, God said my ministry was in the streets and "Souls at any cost" was given to me. I went to much training, studying and applied my self to every area of learning that was offered to me. An instructor once said to me that there is something to be said about a person ever learning: as I looked at her what came to mind the scripture "ever learning but never coming in to" I did not ask for her explanation, I began to defend myself. For truly in the back of my mind I could not allow any one to know more than I did. I needed to know everything. It was my responsibility to put my self in a place and position to learn. And I always believed someone else knew better and was smarter that I was.

A journey from the past. In 1991 my husband and I bought a house finally. I thought at last my dream has come true. I have a house to make my home. It was a miracle how God did it. I began saving a little money, but a miracle by the bank that was not corrected gave us the down payment for the house. Oh yes I tried to tell the bank of the mistake, but the teller told me that they did not make mistakes, I said okay and hung up. I waited about a month because that was how long it took for the closure of the purchase for the house: needless to say after the house was bought, the bank found the error, the banker tried to intimidate me but I refused to be intimidated and told her she would get her money when I deposit by usual deposit in to my savings. God worked a miracle for us.

By this time the three girls were on their own. The two younger ones went with us to Woodbury. It was a challenge: for both wanted to go to school in the hood they called it. One was into football and the other was in to blackness. Needless to say they did not like the school. But I tried to stand my ground and tell them to try to adjust. Everyday their were some kind of story that went on in the school. So I went to check it out. I was met by the teacher of the oldest child she stated that he was just not concentrating, looking out the window all the time. This child would track from Woodbury to Saint Paul just to play football. Finally I told him he had to buckle down and study and let the football go, for he was so close to graduating only one more year. But he fought me tooth and nail with actions of not taking interest in his education. Finally, his graduation came and the school told him he did not have enough credits to graduate with his peers. He ended up taking GED classes across town. In order to finish high school. The younger one I gave in to for he had two more years to go. I would transfer him across town to Central High School, where the vice -principle ended up calling me almost every day for something he had done, fighting or whatever. Finally the day came and He graduated too hallelujah.

Judgment or not:

Somewhere in all of this God pronounced judgment on us/me because prior to all this God had told me to come off my job. I refused to because I said; I couldn't because we had just bought a house we needed my extra income. Even prior to all of this the pastor of my church gave a general prophecy that some of us God will be calling off our job, but I did not want to be one of those people. I also had a dream and was awaken with the words **brazen serpent**. Instead of me putting two and two together: I looked it up as a study lesson never applying it to my life. I didn't have a clue, even after taking sick. A pastor friend asked me if God had told me something and I had not done it? I told him no, I didn't think so.

But while I stayed with the job it folded out from under me. The university was under financial duress and had to layoff many employees. I was one of them: they gave us options to try to find work on our own within the system or take a severance pay. I still tried to hold on, so I looked for work within their system. I found a 6 months full time job. And later landed a full time permanent work so I thought, but the supervisor soon wrote me up as insubordinate and I was out the door within 3 month I believe. But prior to the write up the supervisor called me into her office and told me I was doing a good job and she was pleased.

The next day she had written me up to be out the door the end of the week. When she called me in to read and sign the departure papers she had written, I first refused to sign the paper: stating" this will be on my record would make it hard for me to get another job" She then stated that no one has the right to ask for your records by law. But God told me: "what she did, she had to do quickly". This was relating to the Judas situation of the betrayal. God was still talking to me. I was still fasting and praying, and reading my Bible everyday. But as I reflect on this now, I know I had to pay for my disobedience. So the job fell out from under me and I left the University crying all the way to the unemployment office in humiliation.

Then the attention turned to other situations. I got a job in training as a chaplain at the HealthEast Hospitals, after being fired at the University of MN, but not until I finish the session at the Pneumbra Theater in the "Black Nativity". When that session ended I moved on to apply for the chaplain job-in-training, and got it!! I was happy I was working and doing something that I thought that God was please with.

This training session was 2 years out of my life by choice. Later I was hired at the Region's Hospital as a professional Chaplain Interim, the best job I ever had. Higher pay. Life was good. We were paying bills keeping on top of everything. God spoke to me in a dream that He had not given me the chaplain job at Regions, the new supervisor/head chaplain called me in to his office and told me he could never hire me: I didn't interview well, nor was my education worth the paper it was written on. As I was packing my things because I was there as an interim for 9 months. I was crying and looking through the drawers. I found a tape that stated "God had another plan." So I finish packing and left the building. I was the only black there and this guy was very prejudice, white supremacy, so he tried to get rid of me by insulting my education and my person. He asked the employees in leadership regarding me and I received good reports from all the floors.

In 1994 I left the church I was a member after 4 years and I believe was sent by God to another Church, back into the Baptist setting; I thought Lord what am I doing here. Baptist don't, I'm not Baptist any more, after 10 years of living Pentecostal/charismatic? God show me the church with no bottom, as if it was without a foundation, in the spiritual sense: and that was the reason I was sent there.

Then my husband got this brilliant ideal to quit his job and start a cleaning business and of course I went along with him to support. The enemy threw an iron in the fire and I lost the chaplain job. Not for hire. Went on unemployment and later landed a part time job with the Church I was attending. But it was not enough but God sustained us for my husband business was bringing in some money so we managed. But I wanted to go back to school so I quit the church job and went to work for a music academy and after about 6 months or so, I was fired after getting sick. I contacted Account Temp service and landed part time jobs here and there the last one was a steady job for hirer but I took ill again in 2002 right after my mother died and found myself without a job again. But prior to that I was called back to the HealthEast Hospitals for a professional chaplain job and ended up working in two hospitals until 2001.

In January 2000 I lost my grandchild, what a night mare: I could not believe it: he was 6 years old and gone, it seemed unbelievable unreal, feelings like stop this ride I want to get off, a nightmare perhaps would end if I woke up. I was faced with death starring me dead in the face. A cold numb feeling that would not go away. I tried to be a support for my daughter, but I was unsure of my own feelings trying to get a grip on it all myself.

Then my life took a stumble down hill a series of incidents occurred and it appeared all hell broke loose. We were in jeopardy of losing the house. My husband found someone to help us get on track again to keep the house but he kept wanting to borrow from the house to invest in buying some housing projects. I was against it but I went alone with it. In 2007 we lost the house. We not only lost the house but all the property that we had acquired and had to file bankruptcy.

I am not against furthering your self but I feel there is always better ways of doing things. I asked God to let me not be bitter against my husband and his ideals to prosper our life journey: because all through this I kept asking my husband will this cause us to lose our home. The thing I feared most eventually happened. We found ourselves robbing peter to pay Paul so- to -speak. We filed bankruptcy again for the last and final time I kept telling my self. I told my husband never again will I do this, so far thank God here we are doing okay. We have moved three times since we lost our house each time down sizing but God never allowing me to miss anything I had to give away because it appeared that the more I gave up the more I got back in abundance. My husband has never given up trying to become a business man, he is still trying to make an internet business work. These things were not the only major turning point in my life. The trauma of a missing child:

When my third child was about 13 she and her step-dad had an altercation, one in which she thought I should have intervene but I did not. (Now this dad was the only one she knew for she was about 1 yr when he came into our lives.) As a result she ran away from home after leaving for school the next day she never came home. I felt she was being influenced by someone on the outside expressing their views about what was going on in our home. She stayed away from us for 3 years I looked for her in every place I thought possible, only to find out she was living in a highrise with a formal acquaintance of mine from work. When I found out where she was I went to get her and bring her home, she refused, I was heart broken I thought I had lost her for ever. So I presented this matter to the pastors and we prayed over the matter.

I began looking for ways to get her back, so I thought to send her to her biological dad, which was a huge mistake, that summer she picked up habits of drinking and smoking by her dad encouraging her to do these things. After this I convinced her to come home and she later had this idea to sign up for ROTC, after going through paperwork and series of test, the officer called me at work stating if I knew my daughter was pregnant. I was so hurt

I back-lashed the woman in which she was staying with and all the foolish nonsense that came from the would be grandmother and dad that was 2 years younger than my daughter. After learning of this I tried to support her in every way I could until the baby was born

She went to camp as an counselor. After the child was born she elected to go to a special school, taking up a trade of skilled nursing, after succeeding in this I finally convinced her I loved her and cared for her. I see now that all of this took a toll on both she and I. But with the grace of God we survived she finally opened her eyes to a lot of things only to say four children too late. If and when this single mom get on her feet I could relax a little? 'There is no rest for the weary!!!

The prayers, the thought patterns of uncertainty, trying to grow in God, trying to be a leader in the spiritual calling on my life, trying to take care of family God was right there blessing: God blessed with job, house, furniture, school even through the down tumble., she could not see it, she was truly caught up and some how I was the blame, but thanks to God we both were delivered.

My Steps into Maturity: By the Mercies of God

This part of the book is geared toward the maturity walk of the journey in which I took to come to God with my whole heart. I wanted to say first as I began to grow in God's maturity and grace I began to understand and realize I was something special on His list. I began to understand that as a child: God had always been with me. I was in prayer once and God revealed to me how he was with me from my early age as a child. When I would walk alone in the woods and the lonely roads by myself. How at times, I would go through the trails and tribulations of life struggling with my health problems even up to my broken marriage. The issues I had coming into the process of my calling to the priesthood). Once when I was in prayer at the church I heard a voice say to me "You are a priest".

Needless to say I was a crazy mixed up, fearful child that was trying to become an adult. I had inferiority complexes, racial hangups, insecurities, feelings of inadequate, fear of the dark, fearful of seeing things, fear of being rejected, shyness, divorce issues, emotional issues, my series of illness from childhood to adulthood and even dealing with the lost of my dad (at age 14) and non-belief of women preachers. I started looking for dads in all the men I met young and old. The old to feel like I was wanted and loved from a dad's standpoint. The young to point out that they were all dogs and was no good. I was an emotional wreck headed for disaster but God stopped the runaway train. He loved me and kept his hand on me even though I was not aware of it.

I must attribute some of it to my upbringing. I had a wonderful caring mom, who took us to church. God seemed to always place me with people who cared at home, at school, at church. So here I am today, living to tell about my experiences. I have a testimony about a God who always causes us to triumph (II Corinth. 2:14).

Which I totally believe as I look back on all this: God truly had His hands on me. Since I realize God has truly been good to me over the years, and is still doing great things in my life. I gave my life to the Lord as a young child at the age of 12, I could see myself in those times and interacting always had an interest in God's word we call the Bible.

When I would read the bible it came alive and I could see myself in those times and interacting with those people. But as I grew older and began to understand a little better, I realized that that was not enough to stand as a follower and witness for Jesus. My life style had to change. I had to have a personal relationship with God, not just to know of Him: I had to know Him. He had to become Lord and Savior in my personal life. So after I met Albert and we got married on a Saturday, I went to church that Sunday.

I rode the bus to church. Later that year I rededicated my life back to God in a revival service at Shiloh church.

I have to tell you I slipped from time to time but I repented and now have been on the straight and narrow road of God for over 30 years. I can truly say I love the Lord and He has truly heard my cry. I am a mother of 5 children and 17grandchildren, none of which I thought I would ever have (because of my early childhood illnesses) but thanks be to God, who always causes us to triumph. I now have the opportunity to teach and preach the Gospel to them. What a challenge! I was in prayer once and the Lord told me I was a pastor to my family. That my family was my congregation. I had to realize and understand what a wonderful opportunity and awesome task that I had been given and learn how to walk in the assignment. After all I don't want to go to heaven without my family.

God the Holy Spirit called me into ministry of preaching and teaching in 1985 and I accepted it in 1987, no I was not running. I simple did not understand, if and how God would be calling a woman to preach, not less a crazy mixed up person such as myself, who did not believe in woman preachers and who had never seen one or ever taught that there were women preachers. But none-the-less God confirmed that He was calling me.

After a few conversations with him, I accepted by saying Okay; Lord, if you are calling me you have to open the doors for me and make a way. He did just that. I remember my calling and anointing. While I lie sleeping one night beside my husband. There were nothing unusual about that night, just like any other night. The room was dark but light was shinning very bright. I saw a presence standing at the foot of the bed. I felt his presence I awake and became afraid. I immediately asked if I was dying (my words were Lord am I dying?) He responded lie still I came to anoint you. Then rubbing from feet to head three times. I failed to asked him why was he anointing me. I also tried to awake my husband during this time by nudging and calling his name but he was dead to the world. I could not awake him. After the messenger was finished, he disappeared. The light was gone, I fell back to sleep.

The next day I truly realized what had happened to me as I reflected on the incident. God began to speak to me about my calling. I heard a voice speak to my spirit man "Go ye into all the world and teach and preach the Gospel. Now truly I must say, I don't remember whether it was before or after the anointing but I know I had another conversation with the Holy Spirit expressing to him that I believed that He had indeed called me to teach. I felt I was an anointed teacher, but was He sure I was to preach. For several times after that He confirmed over and over until finally He said to me "We have been down that route before, we will not go down there again." very firmly.

Shortly after that I had an experience of the Lord telling me to read and read and read so I spent all the time I had reading as much as I could when ever I could. I had another experience where He showed me how He would take care of me, if I obeyed Him. I also told Him to tell people for me that I had been called but He told me I had to tell it myself. So I approached my pastor at that time and he said yes I know nodding his head as he spoke. He licensed me in 1988. During this time I fasted and prayed and read my Bible every passing day. The voice of God was so real to me I heard him say I have given you the five-fold ministry. I was not sure if I knew what that was exactly, but when I found it in the Ephesians the 4th chapter and the 11th verse I pounded it in my heart. After which I asked a fellow minister, if God would give someone the five-fold ministry and she emphatically told me no! I got whipped by the Holy Spirit, because He asked me and I know I heard His voice: "Why do you go to man when I tell you something"? "Yes it is I who spoke". (For my sheep hear my voice and a stranger he do not follow (John 10:27).

I still was very naive: I had so many prayer sessions with God so many conversations that I told Him: "I bet He was tired of me". I learned that God expects us to pray and ask and seek him always. He also expects us to believe and trust Him to answer us. In fact, once in prayer, I heard Him speak to my spirit man saying "Expect an answer when you pray". So I do expect Him to answer every time I pray. I also know now that God uses people to bring you answers to your request but I must look for confirmations only from people. I use to get upset when someone said God said and God never told me but He is teaching me in that area as well. {Matthew 18:16b.}. The Bible states: "By prayer and supplication with thanksgiving let your requests be made known unto God" Phil.4:6b.

God has taught me in the area of pride: I have learned that there is a false sense of pride and good pride/that can be labeled as self-esteem. For example as a child I was taught never to ask for things that I could do without or wait until I had the money to buy it for myself. In studying God Word, I learned that I should "Ask and it shall be given" (Luke 11:9 and Matthew 7:7). I also learned that this situation had a lot to do with my dad's own sense of false pride: because He had 5 mouths to feed plus his and he never wanted people to know that he could not or was not providing for his family. My dad was a functional alcoholic, so guess who suffered. But God gave our mom self preservation for she would do what she had to do to take care of us, so our need was not for long.

Through the years I learned that God wants us to Shabach (Praise Him). In October of 1993, I was awaken after a dream, I hear the voice saying to me Shabach Me, Shabach me being repeated over and over. I began to understand if we praise God our blessings comes down. God has blessed in so many ways and taught me so many things. I have been promoted in the spirit realm many times and it has been confirmed by people. God showed me I had to keep an equilibrium with in the things of God, family and life. He informed me that there would be restoring and renewing in my life. That I had to win souls at any cost also given to me in 1993, which let me know I had a responsibility to win souls for the kingdom of God, seeing God doing a new thing in my life as a soul winner.

There were many instances in which God spoke to me and gave me phrases and comments and scriptures and statements concerning my life and spiritual walk with Him. Once telling me I was a Moses and a Job. I learned how these names fit my life, showing me I was a leader and an over-comer.

I was told I had the Spirit of Jesus a (Prophetess, the anointing of Paul, an Apostle, the prophecy of Jeremiah. The Oracles of God. The job of Lazarus, a bishop).

Once in prayer telling me: God would exalt me as He exalted Jesus. And that He loved me as He loved Moses on Mt. Moriah. I had to really come to understand these things and sayings. Some of which I am still working on understanding.

I know the gifts that God has bestowed upon me: As Apostle, prophet, preacher, teacher, prayer warrior, intercessory, evangelist. A soul who would see the world through God's eyes. I learned to have all these things and more because God is in the promotion business and each step goes higher and higher in Him. He would always call me to come up higher. As I began to grow spiritually, God indicated to me that Jesus was the airplane pilot guiding along and when the turbulence come to not be alarmed this was in 1995.

I knew I had a lot of hang-ups but I had to make the conscious decision of whether I wanted God to handle them. I had a choice to hang on to them or allow God to fix them for me. I had to trust God whole-heart-ed and cast all my cares, hang-ups, problems on His well capable shoulders. (1Peter 5:7).

I gave my problems to God and God is still working on my behalf. I know I shall come forth as pure gold. God is not through with me yet.

God placed a street ministry calling on my life and indicated to me that it was a hard ministry but He had it under control. I understand it is not to stand on the street and witness but that it is not behind the four walls of a structured building but to go and compel them to come to God. (This was given during and out of body experience God gave as I watched the Holy Spirit preach my first sermon. I share these experiences with you to confirm that God really speaks to you and how He works with you to accomplish His will, just to note: God is still working with me and through me. I have learned that there is nothing too hard for God and He cares and loves us so very much he is the present help there with us and carrying us through all the time. I like to say earth has no problem that heaven cannot solve.

God told me through his word that I was a watchman on the wall and it was confirmed many times over through the ministry that I have established. The Mercies of God FGBC. God said He would teach me a long time ago and that I could go to school three days: when this was spoken to me I did not understand, what the three days meant, but God has truly taught me and still teaching me.

I cannot begin to tell you all the ways God has blessed. When He said I will open up a window and pour you out a blessing (Malachi 3:10) God does just that. God is not man that He would lie. One of the many blessings is that He opened up the door for me to receive a Biblical Education. I received a Doctor's degree in Pastoral Counseling in 1996). Later I received a two-year scholarship from HealthEast Hospitals for Clinical Pastoral counseling Education (1996-1998). I was later ordained in 1996 with a license to preach and teach the Gospel. I was ordained as a Bishop in 2007. But of course to whom much is giving much is required. I worked as a Interim Chaplain from 1998until 2001, an experience that I would never forget. God taught me to understand that I might have been around those who wasn't fully walking with Him, but no one could take what I knew away from me. My spiritual journal was my own.

The road has not been easy, sometimes lonely, many obstacles and challenges along the journal, but God has been good to me. With God's mercy and Grace a fresh and anew each day I knew I was not alone. God has carried me through it all. With all the challenges and struggles, God has been faithful and a very present help. When my prayer partner began to doubt me then I began to doubt myself, as if I had never heard from God. Things seemed as if it was pressing in on me on every side. I began to cry out to God saying did you want me to open this church if not, I will close the doors and walk away. But in 2007 I believed God told me to close the door and let everything go after two years of paying for storage.

I love the Lord and Savior and I am not ashamed to tell anybody, because He first loved me and taught me how to love His people over the years. I have to tell you I made that teaching a hard task for God, for it was not easy teaching me not to be selfish. He taught me how to give of my time, talent and monies all those areas were hard for me and in some ways He is still teaching me to give until it hurt and if I did I would have the abundance for when I give He gives back to me. I understand now that God does not want me to lack for anything and if I hold on to what He gives I will lack and someone else will also because I would have failed to fulfill a need of someone else. Because it's a give and receive concept: the more you give the more you have, If you don't give you won't receive.

Through my struggles and my encounters with people, God showed me that not everybody was lovable, but I was to show them love anyways, if I wanted to see Him.. When sin abounded grace much more abound according to scripture (Rom.5:20). As I talk about God's blessings and goodness I cannot help to talk about my children. My children are my blessings from God also this Psalm 127:3 tell me so, for God adds blessings and gives no sorrow

(Proverb 10:22). My oldest child has accepted the call of minister on her life I licensed her to preach the gospel. I have baptized 6 grandchildren hallelujah! My oldest son was divorced and remarried and has a lovely wife and baby. I have 5 children and currently all 17 grandchildren are well and doing good. I am very happy for how God had blessed me through them. They are my joy. My oldest grandchild is 27 years old now, as I write this book. I remember being told once, "if I was happy I would soon be sad, because something would happen to change the status of how I feel." But I have learned over the years that I can have what I say.

The Word of God tells me I can. So I speak life over me and not death. I speak life over my family continuously. Because life and death is in the power of the tongue. I speak happiness over our lives. God's Word tells me that He has given me power to tread on the scorpion and has given me power over the enemy. God will rebuke the devourer for my sake. So I have God on my side how can I loose? Besides the Joy of the Lord is my strength and the Greater one lives on the inside of me. Therefore I have a lot to be happy and thankful and grateful about. I don't have to dwell on the things that make me sad because God's love over powers the bad and that's enough to make me happy all the time from the inside out. God has torn down all the superstitions in my live and I am strong in the power of his might. Every day God is building me up to be fit for His kingdom here on earth: for He has made me a king and priest and heir to His throne. He is my Abba Father.

I can continue to talk about God's blessings in my life for the blessings have been many. God have put great men and women of faith in my life to help build me up. He continues to remind me that it's me and him all the way. He deserves all the credit. I have been chastised and scolded alone the way because He loves me and wants me to have character, righteousness and the mind of Christ in every situation. He wants me to build good moral scrupulous while learning to be obedient. I have also learned that sickness and disease come from the evil one and not God however He can get our attention through what we encounter, thereby learning to wait upon Him and listen to His voice and obey his voice, which He teaches us to wait, trust and rely on Him for there is always a lesson to be learned. I have learned to pray His Word, believing and stepping out in faith so that God could heal me. For without faith it is impossible to please God. (Hebrew 11:6).

We must walk in faith believing trusting and relying on God. We must give Him every problem, totally surrender, while casting all our cares upon His shoulders. I have also learned that God has given each of us a measure of faith and it is up to us to make a stand and put our faith trust, to work because faith is an action word and it looks for action in order to work.

God indicates to us to put our faith to work and watch Him work on our behalf. I believe in order for us to receive our healing we must saturate our minds with scriptures of healing every day and began to thank God for our healing. No matter what the situation or circumstances look like or even a report we might have received. For God's Word states who's report will you believe and we should shout with a sounding voice we shall believe the report of the Lord. You might say that's easy for you to say you have not been faced down the barrel of the big C. Yes the big C is devastating; but I have learned to say there is no name above the name of Jesus. Even as I watched my grandchild die of Wills Tumor (cancer of the kidney).

If we hold on, God will deliver! God is always working on our behalf. God is a deliverer. He has delivered me out the hands of the enemy many times. Things I have found myself into and was not proud of and wished I had never done them, wishing I had known what I know now. But God is faithful and just to forgive our sins and cleanse us from all unrighteousness. For His love covers a multitude of sin (I John 1:9, 1 Peter 4:8). God is a faithful and dependable God and has given me many second chances. Now I can truly and willfully say I will not bring any shame to my God's name in thoughts and deeds. I have learned that God loves me and I love Him so together we can do any thing but fail. I have learned that when the flesh rise up and it will, (that's why Paul stated we must put the flesh under subjection and buffet it.) I can call on Him before I act or react, He is my very presence help. God steps right in to help, even to calm me down. For we are to get angry and sin not (Ephesians 4:6).

While on this way to maturity, I believe God has gone with me through dangerous journeys. Teaching me how to live right before Him. I believe that nothing happens by chance. God orchestrates and gives us opportunity to trust rely on and depend on Him through all our experiences. For scripture states everything worketh together for the good of those who are called according to his purpose (Romans 8:28). I believe there is a lesson, to be learned from our mistakes and the biggest one is not to do the same thing repeatedly. I have made a lot of mistakes in my life, a lot of which was out of ignorance and stupidity, but I vow to learn from God's Word. To walk and stay on the path that He leads. For if I do, I will continue to be pleasing to Him. For to please God is my uttermost goal. Eventually hearing him say well done good and faithful child you have been faithful over few come be ruler over many (Matthew 25:23).

When God elevates that's total victory! I am working toward total son-ship, a king and priests and heir to the throne of God (Rev. 1:6).

Over the years God has allowed me to be a lot of things to a lot of people. I have learned to value people of all culture and learned there is only one race and that's the human race. No one should every put another person down by trying to degrade. God states in the Word that all souls are His and what He made was good and very good and that settles that. I will be, glad to see this come about in my life time for when I was a child I used to pray and cry to God about us being so divided as a people. I wondered why do we hate one another without a cause? But God's Word states further that Our ways are not His ways and our thoughts are not His thoughts. Therefore when we hate we are not acting on God's behalf.

We are all equal as humans in God's eyes. God made us all and He stated in Genesis that it was good and very good. If one has more money or wealth than another, this does not make he or she better than the next person. For we all have to die, rot and stink and can't take anything with us, no matter how rich we maybe. For as a Bishop once said "I have never seen a u-haul at a grave sight. '' The Bible tells us that we all have sinned and fallen short of the glory of God. God has no respecter of person and He loves us equally (Acts 10:34). God instructs us to love one another as we love ourselves (John 4:11; Mark 12:31).

For a long time I felt that a white man (what I called our Caucasian brothers, pale pink not white) could never be a friend to any one of the sun burned man. But God has given me beautiful friend ship with my brethren. I have learned to love and cherish their company and their friendship. God wanted me to know that there are true friendship to be found in them.

I believe God has established me as an intercessor and I call myself a prayer warrior and over the years, I have prayed for many people, those of whom I am acquainted and those of whom I am not acquainted, for God has shown me people to pray for I see their faces and I see events and situations that He allows me to pray for. God has given me compassion for people and has shown me the struggles of each nationality, informing me that there is only one race of people: The Human Race.

I have learned that in all people there are some of the same struggles and trails and tribulations, hardships and pain. We need one another as we need God our savior. We should understand our different cultures, backgrounds and ways of doing things. For God has given each one of us gifts and talents, to help meet the needs in our lives as a whole. I believe We must see this is highly important in order for us to get alone with each other, not just tolerate one another but to genuine love and appreciate each other. If we understand this concept of needing and accepting one another then we will not be jealous and have strife among us, we would live as God commanded. I might have used this example before but back in the eighties somewhere around 1986.

God spoke to me regarding the five-fold ministry concept. I had no ideal what to do with it, so I asked a fellow ministry (teacher) regarding this concept I had received and she immediately began to tell me that God does not give one person the entire fivefold ministry. Which I later found out that that is just not true. I believe God scolded me for taking her word over HIS. I now believe that possible she might have been acting out of jealousy or just plain did not understand what she was talking about, but instead of telling me this, she told me I was wrong in what I heard.

My point in telling this is that we need to help one another, share with one another and help nourish and encourage one another in the ministry and above all pray for one another: because we are brothers and sisters in one body, one faith one baptism, seeking one God in the body of Christ. We must pray, believe, trust, rely on God. Once I was visited by a spirit being, I believe he was a messenger from God he was so happy in telling me that he know the name of my church, so I said you do, what is it and he stated The Mercies of God" and then he left my presence.

When I understood what God was calling me for and into. I told HIM I wanted a rainbow church, if ever I was to oversee one as a pastor. I wanted a rainbow of people to worship and fellowship together. I understood that we have different personalities, but equal in being a human being, for when we are cut we all bleed red blood that is needed to sustain our lives. One Saturday morning I was praying and the Lord gave me a vision of the Asian people (i.e. Hmong) how much they were struggling being here in America trying to adjust to our way of doing things, trying to understand our language and missing their families and things they left behind having to learn a whole new way of living, a whole new culture, new concepts.

My heart melted I felt so much compassion, so much empathy for them, trying to understand what they might be going through. (I just didn't want to hear harsh, nasty and hurtful things about them and there were many). I went about every chance I got trying to make friends with them. I learned to not call them all Chinese people, but try to distinguish who was Hmong, Laos, or Cambodian and began to ask questions of their customs and cultures.

I went to immigration meetings seeking to learn all I could, attending community workshops that taught on customs and cultures. I have quite a few Cambodian, Hmong and Japanese friends whom I enjoy very much. I especially enjoy listening to their music and their singing. Sometimes I think about all the experiences that I have had and I wonder if that's not the way the Lord is establishing the Rainbow Church that I had requested, not just structured but in the contact, environment, surroundings, people, places and things. Because God has told me that the church was in the streets not behind the four walls. I believe I am a true Ambassador for God not like others think but how God orchestrated. I want to stay open to whatever God is saying and wherever He is leading me. I consider myself a lover of people regardless of what nationality they may be and if you have a problem with that I suggest you take that up with God through prayer, I dare you to pray about!

When I received a scholarship for chaplain training at the HealthEast Hospital system. I believed God had given me another great opportunity to learn, greet and meet people from all walks of life, nationalities, cultures. He was preparing me for the future of what was to come in my life. I was very grateful for the opportunity and took advantage of it to the best of my abilities. I took on the challenge of performing ecumenical worship services, taught Bible classes to all who would come and visited all hospital rooms and nursing home dorms that I could. Taking on shifts of on- call duties with pager, taking on Black History month as a culture awareness project. I went between all the Hospitals of HealthEast as an on- call emergency chaplain. Here is where I learned to work on my fears of inadequacy, fears of rejection, some of my emotional feelings and hang-ups. This environment put me in a learning position to express my feelings and thought patterns and concerns during my interacting with my peers and people I came in contact.

I learned through this chaplaincy program to own up to and be aware of my feelings and emotions. Being able to talk about what I had experienced while enter-acting with patients and their families and hospital staff made me more aware of myself, causing me to think positive about myself, raising my level of self-esteem and confidence. I learned to ask why and not just accept the things people said and did to me. I learned to say no and not feel bad about saying no. I began to have a better appreciation for life and looked at God in a different light, taking God out of a box. I began to accept people for who they were and in some cases enjoying their different views of God. I learned to see God in other people. I began to pray for people in a better, more informed way and this experience increased my prayer life. God's Word we call the Bible states "man should always pray and not faint:" I learned to understand that to the fullest, experiencing the effect when I didn't. There is always something to pray about. Let me interject and say I had wonderful supervisors, peers, and colleagues during my learning process of hospital chaplaincy that I grew to love and appreciate, a few I still keep contact with.

While on this road to maturity, I believed God had called me to be a pastor another road I had to take coming into the maturity God wanted me to be in my life, part the molding and shaping me in to His character. The very happy and joyous messenger of the Lord told me the name of my church and even in that someone tried to deter me.

He gave me the churches by logs, the churches cleansing scripture passage and logo and motto and church doctrine all came from scriptures.

The messenger told me that the church was not the usually traditional church and that God would work it out, also later telling me that the ministry was a hard one and He had it under control. I prayed and after I believed that I had heard clearly from God. I sought my husband's opinion and others of whom I thought could help in getting started. With much prayer I moved forward inch my inch. There were many struggles along the way, even through my prayer partner and the pastors of her church, who all later found out that they were a hindering instead of a help. By June 1998 the pastoral process began, the Mercies of God FGBC was a seed church setting. I had to build it from the ground.

I failed to ask where was the church located there by thinking it was a spiritual thing.

There were 25 people consisted of my family and a few others. We called ourselves the Mercies Of God Full Gospel Church which God gave us the name, and latter changed it to Mercies of God Furthering God's Business Center which would last for about 10 years. I believed I heard Him say allow the church to be swallowed up by the Unification Church. Now there are those who would not agree with me but I believed I heard Him very clearly but not without questioning. I closed the doors and put the things in storage, later selling and giving the things away by the leading of the Holy Spirit.

We my oldest daughter and sometimes my 2 younger ones went to worship with the Unification Church, there God began another work on/in me, taking me out of my comfort zone and setting me directly into a whole new environment/ a whole difference church worship setting made up on Orientals and Caucasians members, we stayed there for 4 years. I believed I had heard this from God also.

It was fun being a pastor God did a lot of things through the ministry, baptism of my grandchildren, setting up a food shelf, help preparing food and feeding the hungry at the Dorothy Day Center. Traveling visiting different churches. Ordaining my Oldest daughter, meeting new faces all the same time. God blessed us with computers while trying to get the Bible school started But loosing ground with the building. The church ministry lasted for ten years, I must say I enjoyed being a pastor, it has made me a better person I believe this was when I began to see the world through the eyes of God.

During my time as a pastor I was taught and I learned a lot for instance: it had shown me that man is just a mere man subjected to making mistakes, but when we make them and we surly will: we must know we have an advocate with our Father in heaven through our Lord Jesus Christ. I have also learned to put Psalms 23 in perspective in my own life as I walk through the dark valleys of death, dark thinking, depression slopes, icy roads, slipping and sliding. God is there never to leave me nor forsake me. I often reflect on my Mother's words that "to never give up" I know now that I would be giving up on God. I wanted to be a pastor after God's own heart. I wanted to do everything right but of course I am human, so I faulted no doubt many times.

God has taken me many places far above my dreams. Since my trip to Colorado would not be the only place this country girl would go and encounter God's presence. I have traveled to 39 states doing ministry and visiting several states more than once. I have had 7 out of the country trips. I can truly say it was God all the way, causing people to pay my way in more than one case. I have met dignitary and rubbed shoulders with celebrity. I talked with city officials and law makers and foreign leaders. I met with dignitaries and signed a peace mission statement in Israel. I attended a campaign rally for peace on a mission in China, meeting with the governor's wife. I acted as an Ambassador for Peace representing American Clergy leadership Conference in Minnesota while in Japan. I attended an International Inter-religious Federation for World Peace in Washington DC also attending several rallies for peace in Korea. This is just to name a few things that God has done for this poor country girl from rural Arkansas.

I have also had my name written in the" Whose Who" book of New york City, New York. I have been in many honored sessions for awards and recognitions, but through all this, the greatest reward is that I am a Child of God. And that my name is written in the Lamb's book of Life. I am truly grateful for all the great things God has done in my life. God is still doing good things. I am grateful to be able to call myself a child of God.

I tried not to get discouraged, praying all the time concerning church growth, concerning rent for the building, but after hearing the Lord say let the church be swallowed up; I felt at ease about the closing and the moving the things to storage, it was like a burden was lifted up off of me, the struggle was over with trying to keep the building. Then after 2 years I believed I heard God said let everything go. So I did.

I believe God has established me as a prayer warrior and an intercessor over the years I have prayed for a many people, those I know and did not know. God has given me compassion for them and showed me the struggles of each nationality. I have learned that in all people there are some of the same struggles and trials and tribulations, hardship and pain. There are hurting people all over. We need one another. No man is an island. We should take the time to understand and help care and appreciate one another. We should understand our different cultures and background and ways of doing things and embrace the differences. This is highly important in order for us to get along with each other. I believe this is the only way we will learn to accept and appreciate one another with love and to not be jealous of one another to cut down hatred and strife.

On this road through life experiences I came to know God the Holy Spirit. I learned that He is alive and well and is our present help in time of trouble and will lead and guide us in to all truths if we allow Him. He is such a gentleman that He does not force us to do anything. He gives you a nudge and sometimes a push and if you don't take heed He allow you to walk right into your trouble and watches as you fall flat on your face of regret. The old people use to say big dodo. You may ask if God really is like that and I say Yes: for you can grieve the Holy Spirit with your disobedience and because He loves us so He gives us room to falter. The Scriptures tells us that God puts before us life and death and would that we choose life, Deut.30:19. Life with Him as He leads us down a plain guided and protected path. If we wish to stray He allows that to happen.

I experienced the Holy Spirit cloven tongues back in 1985. My family and I joined a pentecostal church setting, (after being raised baptist:) where the Holy Spirit gave me ten different languages and allowed me to hear each one as I spoke them. As I was receiving the tongues I heard a voice say: my tongues are real receive them. God was upon me so fierce that day I cried the whole day while speaking in tongues. From that day on there were no doubt that the tongues were real. There are people who say tongues are not for today, but God gave me proof that they are real. I now pray in tongues and can interpret the tongues some times hearing myself pray with clarity. God gives me visions while I am praying also. I interpreted this as God wanting me to pray for certain people and things during this time. Intercessory prayer is very important!

I recall that day when I received the languages (speaking in tongues) I was asked to help out in the children daycare but the pastor intervened and stated that He wanted me to stay in the main service area. I believe he knew God was going to do something special for me that day. Because prior to that Sunday the pastor had spoke to me during service time once before having someone who was seated in front of me to turn and touch me while he prophesied to me. When the Holy Spirit gave me the heavenly language that was the greatest experience I had ever felt. Since then there have been many experiences.

Prior to that experience I was skeptical and I really couldn't tell you if I didn't believe because I wanted to so bad but really believed that I was afraid to receive. What if they were not real, I kept telling myself. Well any way there was a friend in the old church (Shiloh) I will call it the old church through out this book so if you see it again its the very first church I attended here in Minnesota) which spoke in tongues, she and I would listen to the pastor sermons and go home and call each other to critique the sermons with the Bible as our guide. One day she decided to tell me of her experiences with speaking in tongues by the Holy Spirit. She had been secretly speaking in tongues for quite some time.

You see at that time our pastor didn't want tongues (the spirit language) to be introduced or spoken in his church, nor did he believe in women preachers and my friend was both a preacher and a tongue talker secretly. The Spirit would come upon her so fierce she would faint out by trying to hold Him in. She later told me that she believe the Lord was whipping her for holding it in all that time. She eventually left the church and joined a pentecostal setting and eventually she and I left off talking with each other. I told her I was unsure about it and I was frighten of it because it could be the devil. Guess what! I stayed for years later until God called me out from that church as well.

This pentecostal setting was the church my brother-in-law attended over in Minneapolis where I received the indwelling of the Holy Spirit. After I received the indwelling of the Holy Spirit, I attended my friend's church for a while, also I was instructed by God to acknowledge the Holy Spirit when I stood up to speak to the people, so I did and the more I did He became more and more real and present. He was not just as it or a presence or a force but a living God and entity one of the Godhead Body. The Bible was opened to me with a greater revelations and truths. The Bible became my guide for life.

I wanted to know what the Bible said about everything and if I heard anything that did not agree with my spirit man I was able to guard my spirit man against those contrary words. God began to clean my life and fine tune somethings in my life to make me sharp and in tune and sensitive to the leading of the Holy Spirit. I understood what God the Father was saying when He spoke "Be ye Holy for I am Holy". You know what: I love that scripture and I am glad that I know that it exist, for now it's my witness tool. (I Peter 1:16).

I had heard all my life that a person could not be holy because we were only sin sick creatures saved by grace. But now I understand how contrary that statement is to the Word of God. God wants us to know for ourselves what His word says to us. Behold or see you are a new creature in Christ Jesus, old things are passed away and all things are new. (II Corin.5:17.)

I must believe that I am a new creature in Christ Jesus and can do all things through Him that strengthens me. The older people would put it this way: "you must know down in your know that you know".

God gives me strength to be holy and to walk in holiness. God the Holy Spirit gave me new life a new way way to think and look at life in general and have good life experiences. I have learned to count it all joy, yes even when bad things happened because I had inner joy and peace and no one or any thing could take that away but me only if I wanted it to go. When I learned I had control over what happens in my life. (For life and death is in the power of the tongue). That I could speak to the problem and cause it to line up with God's Word; believing God Word has the final say so in the matter. I call this coming into maturity, oh by the way I am still coming into maturity as long as I still live upon this earth for there is always something to learn. While being and doing pastoral duties I learned that God's mercies truly prevailed over my life. I had to learn how to listen to the Holy Spirit and really obey His leading and unctions.

There have been many incidents I am sure where I did not do that: but once a stranger came to our church worship and told a member that he wanted to speak to me after service, this man scolded me for being long windy and took our money, well I gave it to him by cashing a check that he had stolen, after listening to a sad story that he told concerning he was helping ministries and that he was going out of town and needed to cash his check right away. I ignored all the inner warnings, gut feelings that I was receiving, My spirit man gave me funny feelings kept telling me no but I didn't listen, it turned out that he had stolen some checks from a college near by and was trying to cash them. My bank wanted to close our church worship account thinking that I might have been involve somehow. I learned a very hard and cruel lesson from that incident that I should always follow the leading of the Holy Spirit.

Another situation that I experience cause me to doubt the calling upon my life by not following through with what God had told me instead I asked people for their advice, there is nothing wrong with getting advice but this situation was different. I should have operated in obedience instead I went to others: first a pastor friend and then my prayer partner and my very own husband.

These people whom I valued their opinion deeply. I was stunned and devastated and knocked to my knees so to speak: I was told the name given to me was not a church ministry, but a feeling having compassion for people. I was called to do chaplaincy work, I pursued it but there were no doors opened to me on a long term basic, also that I did not know what I was doing by another and that he would not join the church setting after him telling me to step out. I also was told by another that they had my back later finding out that she also thought I wasn't hearing from God and that I stepped out too early.

Those words burned down to the core of me and really hurt. Because I had to realize that these people who once was encouraging me and telling me that I was procrastinating was those people who really didn't have my back and all was said and done was just lies. The most devastating was about 5 years later my prayer partner telling me that I should not try to get a building and that she felt that I should not even have stepped out these words pierced my heart, it turns out she had been listening to one of her friends, but I had always asked her to be honest with me, sharing my inner thought with her.

These things left me in doubt and fear and wondering alone with unbelief had I really heard from God concerning all this. But my point is always pray and be obedient unto God because I had heard and seen and was given things. Through much prayer asking God was I hearing from him correctly? Should I be doing this and each time I started to walk away from this ministry God some how encouraged and confirmed that He wanted me to stay and not give up So now I pray for a discerning and obedient spirit. I needed to be fully persuaded in my spirit man what I was called by God to do. I will say don't seek man's approval, because jealousy, envy and strife comes in to lead you astray.

I was reminded by God when He first had to chastise me for allowing people to talk me out of what he had given me to do.

God caused me to remember the prophecy I had received some time ago a Pastor friend had given to me that I was truly called to pastor but there were some things I had to go through first. I was also reminded of the time He told me to keep my eyes on Him, prior to starting the church worship of the Mercies of God FGBC. While also being reminded of the saying "It was just Him and me this was during the time I was looking around for someone to help me there were no one. I was also reminded of the scripture that states "I will never leave you nor forsake you." through all this God was trying to build my confidence, my trust and to rely on and in Him, that apart from Him I could do nothing. But I knew I wanted to do nothing without His approval. I wanted Him to order my every step. God caused me to look to Him for my source and resource and reminded me that He was my recourse.

When my grandson died in January 2000 that was such a blow for all of us but my mom died 2 years latter in July of 2002. I thought I WOULD LOOSE MY MIND. I SAID SO OFTEN Lord I don't know what I would do if I lose my mom. I was given the opportunity to find out. The spirit of Fear tried to attach itself to me, there were all kinds of fears, fear of death, growing old, of pain and hurt, losing my mind, the fear of darkness tried to come back, the very thing God had delivered me from years ago.

But God helped me through that, by sending an angel in the form of a person called Rosemary that was teaching a grief class. Who would have thought I would go to a grief class, but I found myself going and talking because I needed someone to listen to my inner feelings that was hard to express. I needed someone to listen and be in the moment with me and not try to fix it, but let me be in that moment, so with much tears and prayer, I made it through. During my time of grief, people would call, greet me with kind words, mostly non-members of the family. Only three of my in-laws called with kind words, no one really knew what to say, again it was God and me. It took God to console me and fill the void I had on the inside of me. I still cry and have my regrets of not being able to call my mom. She was my best friend and confidant.

I feel God moves those we become attached to more than He as a way to keep us focused on Him, because the Word states put no trust in man, no trust in flesh, lean not to our own understanding, and have no other god before Him, but in all our ways acknowledge Him. Sometimes we make our own gods and they began to interfere with what God is trying to do in our lives. Long years ago that very thing happened to me. I had esteemed someone so high, that person could do no wrong and became a stumbling block in my path. One that I regret and wish I could take back all the things that happened but unfortunate I can't. The good thing about that is the Lord God forgave me, cleaned me up and restored me back to him.

I also believed I was headed down that same path again: I had gotten to the point I would not pray without her, I would whisper a prayer or two before bed or going out the door or riding in the automobile, but to spend time quality time with Him alone had diminished. And in my prayer time with her: God told me that he missed me getting alone with Him and I ignored it. I washed it out of my mind as if nothing had been said. Lord I repent right here and now.

When I started back spending time with Him. He said to me where have you been I missed you. God wanted to build my self-esteem and faith in Him. God kept working on me with that. While I was working with the prison ministry: Prison Ministry United we took a trip to the Sandstone prison in Duluth, there were two men and the rest were women in the car. We began to talk about women preachers, one male preacher stated he didn't believe in women preachers and from that conversation I began to doubt my calling and that if it was possible that God had really called me. Now my calling was long before I had ever met this man. I began to pray Lord am I really called to preach and God rebuked me right then and said we are not going down that route again. I have called you and that's final. But what I would do is walk in that for a while and something devastating would come up and I would question it again, and again and again.

I know now that, what I was doing was trying to find people that would confirm and validate me, instead of believing God with my whole heart. Therefore the evil one would set me up each time with someone who didn't believe in women preachers. Why was this constantly happening to me because I wasn't trusting in God the one who called me in the first place. The last time I was confronted with that thought pattern was in 2007 on the internet, I wrote back stating God had called me and if he had a problem with that he should take that up with God for he and I would not ever have this conversation again and I heard no more from that man. This would take me years to rest in the confidence that I was called by God and I didn't have to have man's approval and that I would not get it anyway. I had to learn that it did not matter whether or not I had man's approval. This also had to manifest in my heart for leadership in church worship, "Women Pastors" oh yes man had to put his two cent in this category as well. Every body had an opinion. But what is God saying about the matter. Peter said and I quote: "Man ought to obey God rather than man".

When God called me into His ministry there were many doubts and fears some open and some hidden. I had to trust God to deliver me from them. God preformed for me a special ceremony right in the midst of worship service one night through one of the members of the congregation she prophesied and took my hand as she spoke to me I could feel God's presence around me and I saw a garden in which God and I began to walk in that garden alone and He whispered to me that He loved me and I felt I was His special child and nothing else mattered. There were beautiful indescribable things in that garden that He caused me to see. This time God was telling me that He loved me and would always be with me. The first time the anointing was a beautiful experience also later He caused me to understand what he was anointing me for. I never want to forget the special feelings I had of those events during those visits. There was a song that someone penned entitled "In the Garden as I think of the words to that song I can picture how beautiful the roses were hanging all around giving me a feeling of never wanting to leave the garden nor God's presence. I have a feeling that God would have us feel that way all the time when we are going through and life is treating us mean, harsh and cruel. We can escape to the garden with Him so He put's His arms around us and tells us He loves and cares for us. The Bible tells us many are the affliction of the righteous but God is able to deliver us out of them all (Psalm 34:19).

God would have us trust, rely and believe on Him. I reflect on an incident while working at the University of Minnesota. I would take my lunch break and read my Bible, this particular time shortly after I was anointed to preach the Gospel I walked to the nearby park and sat on the ground to read my Bible. After finishing reading I started back to work for my break was coming to an end I heard a voice speak to my spirit man saying which way will you go? Will you take the long way or will you take the easy way out? So I looked around to determine which way that I would take: If I went through the park the trees would shield me from the sun for it was very hot that day or if I went up the steps to the street there would be no shade. I chose the steps and I made my way up the long brick steps that lead up to the street back to work, but God allowed the wind to blow and the trees to cross and sway to give me shade, it was like a miracle being performed before my eyes. I understood it to mean that if I trusted Him and allowed Him to lead, He would protect and shield and give me what I needed. As I reflect back God has done just that.

Once while in Kansas, I visited with this old childhood friend he and I had made a pack: whenever I needed him I would call, so after the visit I went home and was visited by a sex demon. He was a very very big and very very black and hideous. This sex demon tried to have sex with me to possess my body as I lay across the bed on my back. When he started toward me I called out Jesus but he kept coming nearer and nearer. I called on Jesus again a little louder but he kept coming I called on Jesus louder this time forceful then the demon disappeared. This demon tried to enter me because I had opened the door to him by seeing my friend. While still being married even though my husband and I was separated in mind but not through the eyes of God. I had to repent and ask God for forgiveness. Later God informed me that He did not want me to leave this husband, regardless of the problems we were having. My husband and I reconciled and reunited. Now we are celebrating our 40 years together and our marriage of 39 years. God made it good the second time around.

God deal with me in dreams and visions. Many dreams I have written down, when I think God is telling me something significant for my faith walk. I personally believe God deals with us in dreams because we are too busy to listen when we are awake.. In the book of Joel chapter 2 verse 28 "God tells us that He pour out His Spirit on all flesh and our sons and daughters will prophesy, old men will dream dreams and young men will see visions. Some dreams are with warnings, some dreams bring comfort, some dreams are foretelling but we must take time to ask God about them for clarification. We must seek God for understanding before we write them off as the plate of greens I at last night.

I remember my first vision, I was on a women retreat in Colorado Springs around 1987. We stayed in a cabin in the mountains. My journey of visions began, prior to leaving Colorado. I was given a scenario of being Moses coming down from the mountains after being visited by God. That morning I arose early got dressed and went up into the mountains above where we lodged and sat down on a peak and began to pray. I indicated to God the Father what I had in mind and He told me "now go down from this place" I picked up a long steady stick and started down the mountain. I met a few women coming down the path and one of them yelled and pointed at me "look yawl it's sister Moses!" From that day on everybody referred to me as Sister Moses. I had to inform the rest of the church that my name was not Sister Moses, but some still called me that anyway. But this was a conformation because God had already told me I was a Moses, a Job and a prophet. I truly believe it is the spirit of Jeremiah.

From this Colorado experience, I began to see more and more visions as the Holy Spirit began to instruct and teach me. On the trip home to Minnesota I was praying while riding in the back seat of the van. I had a vision of a man and his son were arguing the son had a shotgun and shot the dad. I said Jesus I don't want to see this! I told one of the leaders and the first thing that came out of her mouth was "did I pray and bind that up?" Wow as I reflect back my prayer partners' son was killed with a shotgun a few years later around 1999. I wonder!!! I recall another vision: It occurred after supper on a Saturday night, I was cleaning my kitchen and there appeared before me a scene of some men in an alley with a baseball bat beating another man and was trying to kill him, As it appeared he was to receive the final blow is when the Holy Spirit rose up strong in me and the heavenly language busted forth from my lips very forceful. I later learned from my prayer partner that there was someone that had been beaten in an alley over in Minneapolis was now in the hospital.

I began to pray more and more because began to see more and more and I realized God was showing me these things so I could pray for the people. I stared to see all kinds of people places and things, once I saw my friend who had died, I believe she was trying to tell me something about my younger son, because he was in the vision also and there was a casket near.

During my early experiences with the Holy Spirit He would show me dreams, visions and would speak to me verbally. I believe this was His way of encouraging and strengthening my faith walk with God. The Holy Spirit would constantly tell me to read, read, then pray pray pray to bring me into a level of maturity and have a relationship with Him where He could use me. The Holy Spirit is my partner and we share a beautiful relationship together. I believe in dreams and visions today and I have a hard time being convenience that it was something that I ate. When I dream I ask God what the dream was about. Sometimes I find out right away and some times later but the Holy Spirit brings it back to my remembrance at the appropriate time. I know God the Holy Spirit does things for a reason because He is constantly trying to bring us into a position of maturity in God's spiritual things. (1Corinth..12:1 &Ephesians 4:17-19)'

I might not understand them all but I believe that everything worketh together for the good and nothing happens by chance. I believe that God speaks to us and works hard to inform us and even warns us but we must listen and obey. When we listens and obeys we are all the better for it, because Gos knows what's best for us. We must trust and obey God. The reason I say God, the Holy Spirit works hard is because He tries to help us get it right, It's not hard for Him. He is such a gentleman that he does not force us into any thing but constantly woos us. **It's hard for us** to receive because we are stubborn, stiff-necked, hardheaded and prideful people. We have the doubting Thomas syndrome. God tried to work (teach, instruct, lead) with us for our own good. I can imagine God trying to open up the tops of our heads and pour in what He would have us to receive if He could. But it doesn't work that way we must be willing to receive freely and then read, pray, meditate on him and His Word.

I know God the Holy Spirit will lead, guide and direct if we allow Him to. I learned that We must listen with our whole heart, mind, will and work hard at the task. Why because the evil one is working hard to tear down what God is building up. We must see and understand that we cannot allow or afford the evil one to steal, kill and destroy. (John 10:10) God has given us the power to pull down strongholds, any imagination that exhausts itself above, to tread over snakes and scorpions and over all the power of the evil one. God's Word also tells us that the greater one lives on the inside of us (1John 4:4, II Corin10:5, Luke 10:19). Why because if you are born again and filled with God the Holy Spirit you have the power.

God the Holy Spirit wants us to be humble, lowly in heart, so He can use us. Have you ever tried to tell your child something and He acts like he wants you to hurry up and finish and He or she keeps saying yea, yea, yea, like they want you to shut up that he or she knows it all. Well I believe we act like that towards the Holy Spirit, we do Him the same way, we grieve Him also. But because of His great love he continues to woo together us unto Him, even when we repeatedly sin God the Father forgives us. They work together to restore us back, when we repent. Scripture states when we repent God is faithful and just to forgive us our sin (I John 1:9). God also remembers that we are but dust Psalms 103:14.

I mentioned that God loves us. Well He hides us in His love and keep us under his wing and hovers over us like a mother hen hovers over her chicks, even when we don't know it. Matthew 23:37). I remember when I was a child around 6 years old (it's a very painful memory) but I believe God walked me through this so I could began to heal deep down on the inside.

I blamed myself for never telling. The guilt I carried was that of feeling that I didn't love my sister enough and therefore all of this was my fault. I also thought that I would also cause great pain. I held this so long that even now only two people know my secret.

But I never understood what was happening to me or why I would just cry at the drop of a pin or feel just violated.

The evil one had me mixed up, even to the point of thinking I preferred women rather than men. I had a hard time enjoying sex with my husband. At one point I was calling my sex relationship with my husband as prostitution without pay. I even wondered how it would feel to be raped. I kept all of this balled up inside of me and it took God to release me and set me free.

With much prayer, fasting and reading of the Bible I was set free. I held on to the scripture that states "who the son set free is free indeed." This is not one of those tell all books for this is hard for me to, share even now as I write for possible for millions to read. I feel exposed, letting the cat out of the bag so to speak. But I understand in order for anything to heal, it first needs to be confessed, revealed and exposed.

I believe God is doing this as I tell my story. We have to keep in mind that this was on my road to maturity. Maturity is a process of stretching, bending, turning, learning receiving, accepting and letting God do the work. Sometimes we like to think the past is behind us and we have out grown those past hurts, fears, angers, secrets, pains, but until we give it all to God and let him deal with them, we are never completely whole. Only God can make us completely whole.

God can fix and mend and heal to the point of nothing missing nothing broken. He is the completer of our lives, man cannot do it alone. I wanted to be free so that God could use me to the fullest for His glory, after all, to serve God was why I was created, to give Him glory in and with my life.

We need to ask ourselves the questions have I totally surrendered to God. Am I holding something back? Am I hiding things in the closets of my mind, thinking perhaps God don't know. Are we sometimes afraid that God doesn't care about what we are going through or that it is not significant and that it doesn't matter to God?

I am here to say let it all go, cast all your cares on Him for He does care. I did and are still casting my cares upon Him. For there were a lot of junk in my trunk. God truly cares and it does matter to Him. Cast all your cares on him for he cares 1 Peter 5:7.

I have learned that if God cares for the lilies of the field and the birds that sings how much more does he cares for us that are made in His image and likeness, Gen.1:26-27; Gen 9:6.

On this road of life experiences to maturity I encountered fornication, adultery, idolatry, ignorance, selfishness, greed, broken marriage, separations, rejections, vindictiveness, low self-esteem, misguided love. Shame, self-ego, false pride. God cared and loved me so that He turned my life around, forgave my past sins and started me on a road with Him. As I list these things, I say no I never committed homosexuality, I never committed drug violations or prostitution. I never went to prison. I never destroyed property, always treated my neighbor right, never was a drunker, but I was a thief, a liar, a sex feign.

I would say I wasn't that bad. I had a reason for everything I did, it was someone else' s fault. As you might know I broke all of God's laws when I broke one. God also states there is no excuse. Excuses does not matter here what does matter is that God loves us so and wants us to repent turn from our evil ways and realizing that fact. Even though most of what I did was out of naive and ignorance, it was still wrong. We can always find someone to blame, but we must own up to the part we played. What we have done and ask God for forgiveness. For all have sinned and come short of the glory of God" Romans 3:23.

Through all this God forgave me and wash all my sins away. I got a clean slate. I know what's done in the past stays in the past and should never rear it's ugly head up again in my life, because I am a new creature in Christ Jesus: old things are past away and I thank God all things are new. How about you won't you let God into your life and give him you past and allow Him to wash you clean and restore you unto Him. Making the present with the future being new in Christ Jesus. God want to change your life turn your life around plant your feet on a solid foundation in Him.

Please allow God to love you as His own as a True Father should. Is there a scripture in the Bible to cover all this? Yes God so loved the World that he Gave John 3:16 and Love covers a multitude of sin Proverbs 34:6 and many more. I am reminded of words to a song; "Love lifted me love lifted me when nothing else would help love lifted me".

God has blessed me tremendously. He has not only cleaned me up and gave me a new start! He as given me five beautiful children, 2 beautiful daughters-in-laws and 17 wonderful grand children.

My Steps to Maturity: Unto thee O Lord Do I put my Trust

I Corinthians 13:13 "And now, abide faith, hope, love, these three; but the greatest of these is love." Galatians 5:6 "For in Christ Jesus neither circumcision nor uncircumcised avails anything, but faith working through love."

Flesh vs. Renewed mind

We need a renewed mind in order to not act out the things of the flesh. We need love to operate our spiritual gifts properly. Even if we have faith we still need love. Faith cannot operate correctly without love. We need our motives pure, clean in order to have a love base walk. We need our motives to be wrapped in love, the love of God: For without Him we can do nothing: John 15:5. I learned over the years that this does not mean that we are robots or mindless but that without God our motives are not pure and we will screw up the situation, and in some cases make it worse. God does not want a robot or a mindless person, but an obedient and willing servant, in order for him to mold and shape us into His workmanship. His masterpiece. God wants to make us kings and priest and heirs to His throne.

We need to be determine to walk in the love of God in spite of what people say or think of us. We must say: "I can do all things through Christ that strengthens me."

We must have an attitude of gratitude of thankfulness. Our attitudes determine our faith walk too. When we start to develop the love of God, through prayer, the walk/life style, the speech /the wording of our mouths all change, we have the attitude of gratitude. When we start developing the love of God, we pray, walk, live and speak differently we have the courage to speak to any mountains in our lives to be removed. We begin to ask God what would He have us to do, no longer desiring to walk in the flesh.

We start applying the Word of God to our life because of what we know not what we have heard. We began to understand that God's Word is very important to our lives and that it is to our advantage to trust, believe and apply it to our lives. Then it starts to become rhema to us and we start to see the necessity to obey whatever God has said in the Word. This is called maturity. it's just like being a parent: when our children began to understand and obey us: We can see them maturing and this makes us happy. God is the same way. We make Him happy when we get it right. No, No God is not there waiting to zap us whenever we get it wrong or miss the mark, but He sticks His chest out when we get it right. Whether we get it right or wrong does not make God love us more or less. God is love and therefore nothing else comes out of Him but love and concern and hope for our lives.

God wants us happy and whole and complete, apart from Him this will never happen. Just love around you, you don't have to go far to see that the world is miserable and in need of something, that something is our God and creator who is reaching out to us in love.

Unto thee O' Lord Do I Put My Trust

God wants us to try harder to get "it "right what is it. The attitudes, the motives, the love, the caring and concern for another, right down to the putting away of our differences of skin color or cultures. We need to learn how to appreciate one another and embrace one another culture differences because there is only one race of people and that is the HUMAN RACE. God made us all, he states in Ezekiel 18:4" All souls are mind and I desire none to perish". Am I speaking one world order, no, but I am speaking Unity in the Body of Christ. Unity in the World in spite of our denominations, our religions and our way of life. God's order. If we embrace one another these words would reign supreme, "United we stand and divided we fall".

I quote the stance that one of our great leaders:" Living for the sake of others". When we realize God's love for us and our love for our fellow man: Then we can say we are truly Kings and Priest and heirs to the throne. One does not need a whole lot of knowledge to cultivate, nourish and take care and apply love. We can just use what we know already that is: To treat others the way you want to be treated.

We need a renewed mind in the Word of God to think the way God thinks loving no matter how unlovable a person is. We need a renewed mind to speak the way God speaks, love and kindness have I drowned thee. I will never leave you nor forsake you". We need a renewed mind to speak the way God speaks about us: "You are more than a conqueror and the greater one lives inside of you. And "I did not give you a spirit of fear but of love, power and a sound mind".

The greater one lives on the inside of us and when I truly learned that I say he I can resist the devil and he will flee and who the son set free is free indeed. I am the righteousness of God and therefore I have power over all the power of the evil one because God has given me that power. We must realize that all of God's promises are yea and amen. But only if we apply them to ourselves. If we never come into maturity, we make God out of a lie in our lives. We will never become all that He would have us to become. We need a renewed mind in God's word. I quote a saying of a writer:" Each day may Christ become clearer, His cross dearer, our hope nearer.

Life Experiences in Ministry

Mercies of God FGBC
580 Prior Ave.
St. Paul, MN
Founder/ Sr. Pastor/Lecturer

St. Anthony Block Club
770 University Ave. St. Paul
Guest Speaker

Full Gospel Witness
Pastor Rose Mullen
1522 Upton Ave. Minneapolis. MN
Guest speaker

Community Missionary Baptist Church
Minneapolis, MN
Guest Speaker

Sabatani Center- Minneapolis, MN
PMU-A Team Meeting
Guest Speaker

Peace Hill Baptist Church
Selby Ave., St. Paul, MN
Guest Speaker

The Living Word Church & World Outreach Center
St. Paul, Mn
Speaker/Teacher/Assoc pastor/Junior Church

Morning Star Missionary Baptist Church
St. Paul, Mn 55104
Bible Lecturer/Speaker/Associate Pastor

Faith Deliverance Center
Minneapolis,Mn
Speaker/Bible lecturer/Member

Bold Gospel Deliverance Ministry
Associate Pastor/Secretary/Speaker
Guest speaker/Music provider/Tutor for GED
Prison Ministry United for varies Prisons
Moose Lake, Lino Lake, Shakopee Women, Faribault Max.
Hennepin Co. For Women, Hennepin Co. for Juvenile,
Hennepin Co. Home School
Ramsey County Correctional Facility and Colorado,
Wisconsin State Prisons

Highest Praise Ministries
Minneapolis, MN
Guest Speaker/Music

Bread of Life Christian Center
620 w 34th Street
Minneapolis,MN

Minneapolis Unification Church
Minneapolis, MN
Guest Speaker/Lecturer/Music

Bethesda Baptist Church/American Clergy Leadership
Conference
Minneapolis, MN
Guest Speaker/

River of Life Christian Center
Guest Speaker

Hearts Desire Ministry
500 Dale Street
St. Paul, MN
Guest Speaker

Living Water Christian Center
Kansas City, Kansas
Guest Speaker/Music

Praises For Promises
Ass. Facilitator /Speaker
600 University, St. Paul, Mn

Bethesda Care Center
HealthEast Hospital System
Lecturer/Service director/Music/Chaplain

Missionary and Ambassador for Peace Touring to other ministries of over 40 states in the US and Around the World through the American Clergy Leadership Conference: Such Places as The Demilitarize Zone; Seoul, Bushan, Korea; Beijing, China; Japan; Rome, Italy; Bethlehem, Jerusalem, Capernaum, Darby, Jordan, Nazareth, the Dead Sea, Israel.

Mercies of God Full Gospel Church

"The Lord is good to all: His tender mercies are over all His works". Psalms 145: 9

Printed in the United States
By Bookmasters